Reflections
OF
IRELAND

Reflections
OF
IRELAND

Patricia Tunison Preston

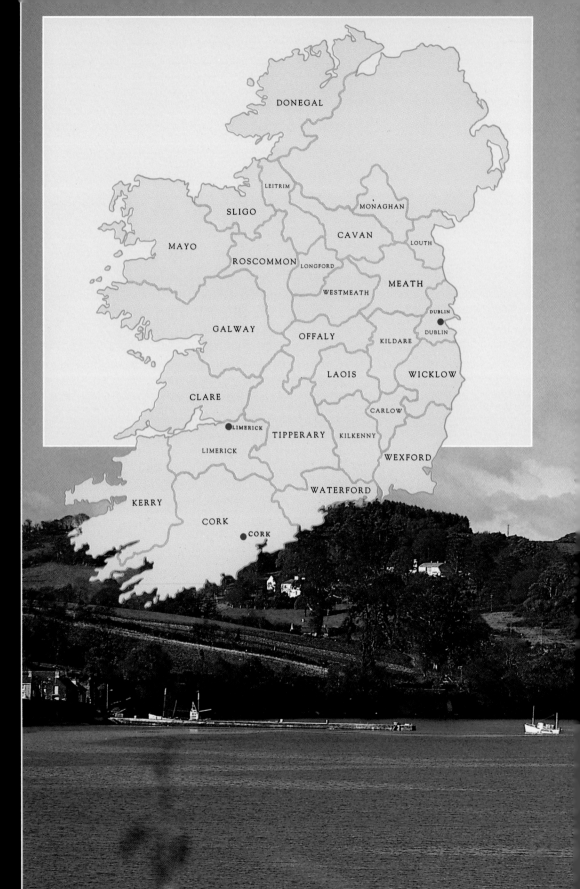

Text
Patricia Tunnison Preston

Design
Alan Hamp

Photography
Tony Ruta
Ron Sandford (Black Star)

Photo Editor
Annette Lerner

Project Director
Sandra Still

CLB 2546
This edition published in 1992
by Eason & Son Ltd.,
66 Middle Abbey Street,
Dublin 1, Ireland.
© 1992 Colour Library Books Ltd.,
Godalming, Surrey, England.
Printed and bound in Singapore
All rights reserved
ISBN 1 873430 019
EASON & SON LTD.

CONTENTS

— 6 —
The Treasured Isle

— 56 —
Etchings of Time

— 86 —
The Land of
Heart's Desire

— 114 —
Wealth of Words
and Music

— 122 —
Enduring Crafts

— 144 —
Passion for Sport

— 158 —
Lasting Impressions

Above: *a cheerful café in Ballyporeen, County Tipperary.*
Right: *haystacks on Slea Head on Dingle Peninsula, County Kerry.*

The Treasured Isle

In all of modern history, Ireland has always been set apart, an island totally surrounded by water, beyond the far reaches of Continental Europe and well west of Britain. For many centuries, this little island was a distant outpost, perched on the edge of the world, and so far from the center of civilization that the Romans did not even bother to conquer it.

In recent years, with the discovery of life beyond the Atlantic, Ireland's role has changed, from a far off frontier to a link between the Old World and the New. Ireland is a gateway between Europe and the United States, a stepping-off point for transatlantic flights, a buffer zone of four million friendly and good-humored people. It is not uncommon for the Irish themselves to refer to the western outreaches of County Kerry as "the last parish next to America."

As a member of the Common Market, Ireland is slowly becoming enmeshed in the European Community, getting into the thick of things in a new economic alliance. Yet Ireland steadfastly clings to its own unique identity – a small and spunky island, rimmed by the ever-changing and ever-challenging waters of the Atlantic Ocean and the Irish Sea.

The total area of the island is 32,523 square miles,

Above: *a foxglove in Rossdough, Co. Waterford.*

or about the size of the state of Maine. The greatest width of the country is 189 miles, and the greatest length is 302 miles. It is small enough to drive from its southern tip, Mizen Head, to its northernmost point, Malin Head, in a day or two, but few people ever do. To rush through Ireland at fifty or sixty miles an hour would be to miss the very essence of this treasured island.

The topography of the land is shaped like a saucer – a broad limestone plain in the center, rimmed almost completely by coastal mountains and highlands. The central plain, which is largely bogland and farmland, is broken in places by low hills. It is also dotted by hundreds of lakes, rivers, streams, brooks, and waterfalls.

Although it is diminutive, Ireland is intensely complex and varied – a combination of thirty-two different counties. Twenty-six of these counties comprise the Republic of Ireland, the focus of these pages; and the remaining six counties constitute Northern Ireland. And no two counties, cities, or stretches of countryside are the same; it takes weeks to get to know all of Ireland. Some say that it takes years, or maybe even a lifetime.

Above: *Dublin's River Liffey, which rises in the Wicklow Mountains.*

Left: *O'Connell Bridge, the heart of Ireland's capital.*

What is it that makes the island of Ireland so different, so unique? The answer is that there is no one answer. Ireland is an experience, or indeed many an experience, each one different for every person who sets sight on the kaleidoscope of green fields, or treads along endless bog roads, breathes the sweet wildflower-filled air, feels the soft pervasive raindrops, hears the foot-tapping cadence of traditional music, joins in the spontaneous and coalescent laughter, and indeed comes to be enchanted by the land and its people.

For many, the best of Ireland is embodied in the capital city of Dublin – a combination of old and new vistas, a hectic yet relaxed atmosphere. Home of an international airport and seaport, it is the seat of the Irish Government, headquarters of dozens of banks, financial institutions, and major international companies, and the hub of great theaters and museums, and yet it exudes a hometown environment, with a friendly pub or two on every corner.

Sitting on the edge of the Irish Sea, straddling both sides of the River Liffey, and rimmed by a semi-circle of inland mountains, Dublin is indeed a "fair city," as the old ditty says, "where the girls are so pretty." Beyond that, the streets are wide and well-swept, parks and pedestrian areas are plentiful, and green double- decker buses seem to glide with the ease of bicycles beside the congested quays and along kinetic thoroughfares like O'Connell Street and College Green. Motorists, often squeezed to the side, vie for space with horse-drawn carriages and the occasional donkey cart.

Above: *evidence of Dublin's Georgian era abounds.*

Left: *a 1960s' color covers an elegant Georgian door.*

Above: *the restored stonework of the Gothic-style doorway of a Dublin church. Dublin is particularly proud of its many churches.*

Severe Georgian sash windows are reflected in the fanlights of a Georgian door in Fitzwilliam Square, a Dublin showpiece.

Best of all, this is a compact capital city, easy to negotiate on foot. Architecturally, Dublin is a good example of a largely intact eighteenth-century Georgian city. The landmark public buildings, sweeping avenues, and graceful squares are surrounded by rows of brick-fronted townhouses, each with its own unique door. Often referred to collectively as "The Doors of Dublin," these elaborate entranceways have come to symbolize Dublin in all its past and present glory. Some doors have fanlights, arches, columns, or sidelights, others have decorative brass bells or knockers. Each is painted a different color – pink, red, yellow, green, lavender, and so on – a rainbow of classic individuality.

In Dublin, conviviality is the norm, and all of the inhabitants seem to know one another. Dubliners, young and old alike, rarely walk down a single street without stopping to acknowledge each other or give a friendly wave or greeting. And, after a few days, visitors seem to fall right into the pattern of a few affable words, a nod, a smile, or even a wink in some direction.

The average Dubliner speaks English and speaks it well, albeit with his or her own special lilting accent. It is often said, in fact, that the best enunciated English in the world is heard in Dublin, especially in literary and scholarly circles. Some Dubliners, on the other hand, have their own special way with words, often dropping consonants and elongating vowels, a sort of " Dublinese." The word "ha'penny" for half-penny" (as in the city's "Ha'penny Bridge") is a good example.

With a recorded history going back at least a thousand years, Dublin has been home to a roster of citizens as diverse as its own urbane charm – from literary figures such as Jonathan Swift, Oscar Wilde, George Bernard Shaw, William Butler Yeats, Sean O'Casey, and James Joyce, to actress Maureen O'Hara, Olympic runners Ronnie Delaney and Eamonn Coghlan, and rock concert organizer/fund raiser Bob Geldof.

Dubliners believe in working hard and in playing hard, with over thirty golf courses, two racetracks, polo fields, horse and dog tracks, and dozens of other sporting venues within easy reach of the city. The nearby beaches and harbors of Dun Laoghaire, Sandycove, Dalkey, and Howth are all less than a half-hour's drive.

Even during the work day, Dubliners are adept at

High Victorian plasterwork, begonias and conifers enhance a pair of Dublin windows.

Right: *Dublin's St. Patrick's Cathedral, the longest church in the country.*

taking time out – time to refresh themselves and time to talk. In characteristic style, they even hum a song that says it all, " Dublin can be heaven, with coffee at eleven. . . . "

Without a doubt, "the place" to go for coffee is Bewley's Cafe on Grafton Street – a quintessential Dublin institution. Founded in 1840 by a Quaker named Joshua Bewley, this three-story coffee house is open every day, frequented by rich and poor, young and old, local and foreigner alike. Step inside, and inhale the rich aromas, gaze at the stained glass windows, take a seat at any one of the many family-style tables, sip a cup of Bewley's brew, munch on a "sticky-bun," and chat with customers seated to the right and left. Now, that's real Dublin!

Another trademark experience of Dublin is a stroll around St. Stephen's Green, a seventeenth-century pedestrian park covering twenty-two acres in an almost perfectly square layout. A verdant haven in mid-city, it is simply called "The Green" by Dubliners,

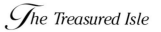

Above: *chandeliers in Dublin's grand Shelbourne Hotel.*

Right: *a lamp-bearer for Dublin's Shelbourne Hotel.*

Facing page: *the statue of Daniel O'Connell, Dublin.*

Below: *a fine door knocker, one of many found in Dublin.*

who flock to enjoy the flowers, trees, wildlife, fountains, ponds, and open-air lunchtime concerts. It's an incomparable place to stop for a while, sit on a bench, lean back, and savor the sights and sounds of this open-hearted and gregarious city.

It's a hard city to leave, but those who do usually head to Cork, the ebullient metropolis of Ireland's southwest coast. It has been said that Cork is the Irish version of Manhattan, and indeed it is built on an island, but that's about the only similarity.

Above all, Cork is Ireland's "river city." Although many Irish cities and towns are located on or near rivers, only Cork is so closely identified with its river, the Lee. Even Cork's official anthem sings the praises of the river, "On the Banks of My Own Lovely Lee."

Cork sits between two channels of the river, with a "midtown" area that spills over onto the north and south river banks, with no fewer than sixteen bridges spanning the narrow strips of water. Many of the bridges are so short that they hardly seem to be crossing over water at all. Getting around this city means frequent criss-crossing from one side of the river to the other. Indeed the Lee is the mainstay of Cork.

To add to the challenge of getting around Cork, the majority of streets are one-way. Most sections are at sea level, but St. Patrick's Hill, on the north bank of the Lee, is as steep as any street in San Francisco. A climb to the top of this hill, however, has its own reward – a sweeping view of the Cork skyline.

A bright porch light and a strong rail, indications of dark nights and wild weather in rural County Cork.

Right: drystone walls and rich pastureland in County Cork countryside. Cork is the largest of Ireland's counties.

Once a great house dominated the Mallow countryside in County Cork. Today only a ruin remains, nestling amid deciduous woodland near the River Blackwater. Mallow was once the only place where it was possible to cross the Blackwater, as for a long time it was the only town in the Blackwater Valley that had a bridge.

It's no wonder Corkonians aways seem to be bustling, moving excitedly from one street to the next. Cork people have even developed their own patois to match the mood of the city, a fast-paced, sing-song, and up-and-down way of speaking. It's almost musical to the ears of out-of-towners.

Because of its unique layout, its relatively remote location, and the plucky attitude of its citizens, this city has asserted a remarkable independence from outside authority over the years, gradually earning itself the title of "Rebel Cork." This is carried through to this day, as Corkmen go out of their way to do things their own way, differently from Dublin or the rest of the country.

This is why a day or two in Cork is like time spent nowhere else in Ireland. Even the architecture is unique, from the highly ornamented French Gothic cathedral, St. Fin Barre's, named for the sixth-century founder and patron saint of the city, to St. Anne's Shandon Church, an early-eighteenth-century edifice famed for its giant pepperpot-shaped steeple, topped by a gilt ball and a fish-shaped weathervane. This church, which stands out on the horizon of the city's north side, is also renowned for its belfry, with eight chiming bells injecting melodious signals into the commercial hum of Cork.

Cork is a city of wide and curving thoroughfares, such as the Grand Parade, the South Mall, and St.

Left: *pastures near Mallow, a graceful eighteenth-century spa town in County Cork.*

Above: *bracken runs down to the water in County Cork, where a solitary boat sails.*

Patrick Street, called simply Patrick Street by the locals, as well as narrow passageways, with names descriptive of their origins – Mutton Lane, Market Lane, and Churchyard Lane. Other landmarks distinctive to Cork include rows of eighteenth-century houses with bow-fronted windows; a central produce-market arcade, known variously as the City Market or the English Market, with a tradition dating back to 1610 and still thriving to this day; and the Father Matthew Statue, a memorial to the nineteenth-century "apostle of temperance," situated on Patrick Street at Patrick Bridge, smack dab in the middle of the city – and surrounded by dozens of pubs. Typically Cork.

Cork's greatest landmark, the famous Blarney Stone, is outside of the city, six miles to the northwest. In many ways, the Blarney Stone is to Cork what Big Ben is to London, the Eiffel Tower to Paris, the Empire State Building to New York, or the Golden Gate Bridge to San Francisco. Just about everyone in the western world has heard of the Blarney Stone and associates it with Cork and with the Emerald Isle.

This unique stone is part of fifteenth-century Blarney Castle, the centerpiece in a village of the same name. Originally the stronghold of the MacCarthy clan, all that remains of the castle today is a massive eighty-three-foot-tall, square-shaped keep, or tower, with a battlemented parapet. The fabled stone is wedged underneath the battlements, and, in order to kiss it, visitors must lie down and bend backwards over the edge. The risk is not nearly as great as it sounds – this hallowed sector of the castle is fully

A wayside shrine in Adare
village, County Limerick.

Right: *King John's Castle
Limerick, County Limerick.*

protected and supervised by a competent staff, but
the mystique draws thousands of anxious visitors
every day.

The hardest part of the whole experience is
climbing up the dozens of steps to reach the parapet,
but legend has it that the reward is great for those
who make the effort, since kissing the Blarney Stone is
supposed to convey eloquence in speech or "the gift
of the gab." It only seems appropriate that a stone
with such loquacious powers should be a part of the
Cork experience.

Like Cork, Limerick is also a city shaped and
influenced by a river, the Shannon, longest of all rivers
in Ireland or Britain. Because of its position on the
Shannon, Limerick has always been an important port,
dating back at least to the tenth century. Today, of
course, it is the gateway city for the airport that owes
its name and location to the river, Shannon Airport.
Thanks to the duty-free manufacturing zone at
Shannon, the Limerick area is a hub of foreign
industry and investment, the most international of all

Irish cities outside of Dublin.

Prettily situated, Clifden lies in the Connemara region of County Galway, on the wet but beautiful west coast of Ireland. It is the principal town of the region and one of the loveliest.

Much of Limerick's architecture is similar to that of Dublin and dates back to the Georgian period, set off by wide streets and avenues lined by brick-fronted townhouses. For many years, Limerick was not quite as polished or as well-maintained as Dublin, but recent urban renewal work has perked up Limerick dramatically, with restoration of the original city walls and medieval quarter near the river. Crumbling old buildings have also been "born again" and transformed into mid-city market places and shopping centers, designed with façades that are in harmony with the city's eighteenth-century streetscapes, yet totally modern inside with state-of-the-art people-movers, geometric skylights, and multi-level car parks.

Of all the cities on Ireland's west coast, Galway stands out as the most characteristically Irish, with its narrow streets, medieval arches and alleyways, and cobblestone lanes. Situated at the mouth of the Galway River near the northwest corner of Galway Bay off the Atlantic, it has always been a great seaport. By the thirteenth century, it was trading regularly with Spain, France, and Flanders, as well as with distant Baltic lands.

The waters recede from a tidal basin north of Galway Bay to reveal the pi-colored test of a sea urchin – a solitary orb on a gold and green raiment of seaweed.

In those early days, the city came to be dominated by a group of fourteen wealthy merchant families, mostly of Anglo-Norman origin, who ruled it as an oligarchy. In time, these families (Athy, Blake, Bodkin, Browne, Darcy, Deane, Font, French, Joyce, Kirwan, Lynch, Martin, Morris, and Skerret) became known as "The Tribes of Galway." By far the most important were the Lynches, who not only gave the city its first mayor in 1484, but eighty-three others during subsequent years. Many of Galway's present commercial shops and structures still bear the names

Left: *reading the news in Galway city, County Galway.*

Below: *playing "mothers," Roundstone, County Galway.*

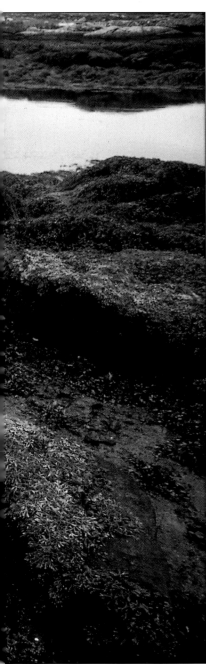

Mending fishing nets in Kilronan on Inishmore Island, County Galway.

Below: *salty air takes its toll on an old bicycle in the Aran Islands, County Galway.*

or have some connections with the original fourteen so-called "tribes."

In contrast to the preponderance of older buildings, Galway boasts one of Ireland's most modern and mammoth religious sites, the Cathedral of Our Lady Assumed into Heaven and St. Nicholas, opened in 1965. It stands out on the Galway skyline like a mini-version of the Vatican, with a façade of Connemara marble and limestone, measuring nearly three-hundred-feet long and one-hundred-fifty-feet wide, with a rotunda-style roof. A few feet away is a

landmark of a different sort, the Salmon Weir Bridge. Rarely does anyone pass by without leaning over this old stone span to watch in amazement as an endless parade of silvery salmon leap into the air as they go up the river to spawn.

But the sight that consistently draws the most attention is Galway Bay, particularly on a clear day at sunset hour. Drive west of the city for the best views, as the amber and golden sunset glistens on the choppy blue waters and illuminates the rocky coastline. The Aran Islands stand out on the horizon

like three giant whales at rest. No wonder people travel from halfway around the world "to watch the sun go down on Galway Bay."

On Ireland's southeast coast, two cities, Wexford and Waterford, reflect a wealth of Viking traditions. Wexford, a name evolved from the Norse "Waesfjord," hugs the Slaney River, while Waterford, from the Norse "Vatrefjord," sits on the banks of the River Suir. Both cities still have remnants of their original stone walls, built by the Vikings.

True to its origin and shape as a walled town, Wexford is so compact that its main street is closed to vehicular traffic during business hours, and some side streets are so narrow that there is barely room for two people to shake hands in the middle.

Waterford, on the other hand, is more spread out, although pride of place still belongs to Reginald's Tower, built in 1003 by a Viking governor of the same name. Reputed to be the oldest tower of mortared stone in Europe, this huge round structure sits beside the river on the central Mall, dominating the Waterford skyline with a conical roof and walls that are ten feet thick. Although much that is medieval remains in Waterford, the city's main claim to fame today is that it is the home of the Waterford Glass Factory, the leading producer of handcut crystal glassware in the world.

Turning inland, one of Ireland's most intriguing cities is Kilkenny, situated on the banks of the River Nore. Often called the "medieval capital of Ireland," Kilkenny was chosen as a venue for several Irish

A tangled skein of fishing tackle on a quayside in the Aran Islands, County Galway.

Right: *a black pony and white walls, typical Aran Islands sights, County Galway.*

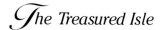

Facing page: *the town of Enniscorthy on the River Slaney in County Wexford.*

Right: *marigolds spill out over a windowbox in Gorey, a small town in County Wexford.*

Below: *a sleek young thoroughbred grazes near Gorey, County Wexford.*

parliaments during the fourteenth century. Centrally located and convenient to Cork, Limerick, Dublin, Waterford, and Wexford, it also served as the capital of Ireland for a brief period, 1642-1648.

Today the city revolves around two great landmarks, St. Canice's Cathedral, completed in 1260 on the site of a sixth-century monastery founded by St. Canice, and Kilkenny Castle, dating back to 1172 and the home of one family – the Butlers – for almost six hundred years. From its sturdy corner towers, three of which are original, to its battlements, Kilkenny Castle retains the lines of an authentic medieval fortress and duly sets the tone for the entire city.

A well-preserved and very walkable enclave,

Left: *the popular family resort of Courtown Harbor, a seaside village in County Wexford.*

A windswept John Barry stands firm in bronze on Wexford town harbor, County Wexford.

Kilkenny has not varied much with the passing of the centuries. The main thoroughfare, High Street, which changes its name to Parliament Street in midstream, is home to a string of medieval architectural gems, such as The Tholsel, otherwise known as Town Hall or City Hall, and originally a toll house or exchange; and Rothe House, a wealthy merchant's house with an arcaded front, timbered ceilings, and a cobbled courtyard. Nearby are the Shee Almshouses, built to provide housing for the poor; and Kyteler's Inn, the oldest house in Kilkenny, once the home of Dame Alice Kyteler, a lady of great wealth who was accused of witchcraft. A walk around town leads to a network of narrow streets and arched laneways, many with original graphic names, such as Pennyfeather Lane, Horseleap Slip, Butter Slip, New Building Lane, and Pudding Lane.

Waterford city, the heart of County Waterford, lies on the south bank of the River Suir and dates from Viking times. In 1170 Strongbow took the town, after which it became second only to Dublin in its importance as an Anglo-Norman stronghold.

37

Above: *an antique bell in Inistioge, County Kilkenny.*

The Passage East area in eastern County Waterford.

Right: *the peaceful fishing harbor of Dunmore East, an angling resort that lies at the mouth of the River Suir in eastern County Waterford.*

Above: *antirrhinums in full bloom, Rossdevga, County Waterford.*

Ireland's other major cities and towns, from Castlebar to Cavan, Donegal to Dundalk, and Tralee to Tipperary, not to mention Sligo, Westmeath, Longford, Athlone, and many more, have still other stories to tell, other sights to show, other experiences to reveal – certainly enough to fill several volumes. And yet, to most aficionados of Ireland and things Irish, the cities are only the beginning, the tip of the territory. It is the countryside that holds the true essence of Ireland.

Inevitably, it is the countryside where the imagination reigns supreme, where the soul basks in nature's beauty, where the urge to sing or hum a lilting tune is irresistible, and where peace pervades the air. Deep in the countryside, there are no garish billboards, no fast food chains, no toll booths, no freeways, no traffic lights, no public address systems, no deadlines, no urgencies, no nonsense. Instead, there are ever-changing vistas of verdant valleys, fertile farmlands, and silvery seacoasts, with occasional rock-streaked hillsides, finger-shaped peninsulas, budding forests, floating islands, lake-rimmed boglands, nomadic sheep, meandering dairy herds, and rosy-cheeked children.

Killarney, celebrated in copious prose, poetry, and song, is home to three undeveloped and unpolluted lakes, on Ireland's southwest coast in County Kerry. No condominiums, cottages, or trailer parks are perched along Killarney shores, only lush foliage such as rhododendrons, azaleas, magnolias, camelias, hydrangeas, and tropical ferns. At almost every turn, there are specimens of Killarney's own botanical wonder, the strawberry tree, as well as eucalyptus, redwood, and native oak. The only permanent residents of the lake district are indigenous wildlife, including a rare herd of native red deer, plus the sleek, all-black Kerry cattle, and more than one hundred species of birds.

No cars are allowed in the parklands of Killarney, only horse-drawn jaunting cars, the traditional mode of local transport. A ride on a jaunting car is an experience unique to Killarney – passengers sit on either side of an open cart and the driver, known locally as a "jarvey," is perched up front. He not only guides the horse but also provides a running

Left: a copper beech in Kilkenny, County Kilkenny.

Kilkenny Castle, the pride of Kilkenny city, County Kilkenny.

Facing page: *Sneem River, a salmon river, runs high after a shower in County Kerry.*

Right: *a brisk trot near Killarney National Park, County Kerry.*

Below: *immaculate Georgian houses line the road in Inistioge, County Kilkenny.*

commentary, complete with local legends, and, with the slightest encouragement, an appropriate song or two. The clip-clopping sound of horses' hooves has become synonymous with this tourist mecca.

Killarney is the starting point for one of Ireland's most scenic drives, a twisting path around the mountains, cliffs, boglands, beaches, and shorelines of the Iveragh Peninsula, more commonly known as The Ring of Kerry. The narrow road follows the full circuit of this 110-mile finger of land, reaching out into the Atlantic Ocean and passing a panorama of palm-tree-lined resorts, tumble-down, thatched cottages,

Carefree smiles in the summer rain – visitors to Killarney National Park, County Kerry.

Right: *Knockagallaun in the Slieve Miskish Mountains, southern County Kerry*

abandoned fortresses, and thriving little towns with melodic names like Killorglin, Glenbeigh, Parknasilla, and Kenmare. Just north of The Ring is the Dingle Peninsula, similarly jutting out into the ocean, but with less-trod roadways and a more remote allure. Many visitors get lost on the Dingle Peninsula, but they are never in a hurry to find their way back.

County Clare, to the north of Kerry, is a rocky spectacle – rocks of all sizes and shapes, strewn on the ground, above the ground, and indeed embedded beneath the ground. In the heart of Clare is "The Burren," a one-hundred-square-mile region, which, to no one's surprise, means "great rock" in the Irish language.

The Burren is a unique lunarlike area of bare carboniferous limestone enveloping farflung little towns like Corofin, Ennistymon, Lahinch, Lisdoonvarna, Miltown Malbay, and Ballyvaughan. Massive sheets of rock, jagged and craggy boulders, crusty underground caves, ancient dolmens, and prodigious potholes are visible for miles in a moonscape pattern, yet this is also a setting for fast-flowing lakes and streams, pockets of hard-won

Facing page: *lush vegetation, typical of southwest Ireland.*

Above: *western dwarf gorse flowering in County Kerry.*

Last of the line, a Doolin crofter in western County Clare.

The mighty Cliffs of Moher in County Clare. Walking close to the edge of these cliffs is inadvisable, since the rock is liable to crumble and below lies a drop of nearly 700 feet.

Above: *anchor chains on the Aran Islands, County Galway.*

Below: *stripped wood on Inishmore, the Aran Islands.*

Right: *tools of the trade on Kilronan dock, Inishmore. Of the Aran Islands in Galway Bay, Inishmore is the largest and Kilronan its main port.*

farmland, a wild, frothy Atlantic coastline, and intriguing placenames such as Pink Cave, Puffing Hole, Intrinsic Bay, Chimney Hill, The Elephant's Teeth, and Lovers' Leap.

At the edge of Clare, holding back the ocean waves, sit the mighty Cliffs of Moher, rising to 668 feet and extending for five miles along the coast. On a clear day, all of Galway Bay and the Aran Islands can be seen from this remote and unguarded precipice.

Those who have never been to Ireland sometimes conjure up images in their minds of what the Emerald Isle must look like. To match their dreams, there is no better place than Connemara, in the western half of County Galway.

Connemara – even the name sounds magical, although this remote region does not have any outstanding landmarks, no great buildings, or any unique national monuments. Connemara is simply Ireland as it used to be.

The coastline is indented with little bays and inlets, small harbors, and beaches. At almost every turn, there are lakes, waterfalls, rivers, and streams, while a dozen purplish mountains, known collectively as the "Twelve Bens," rise at the center. All of this is interspersed with rock-strewn land and flat fields of open bog, and rimmed with gorse and heather, rhododendrons and wildflowers.

At every turn, there are simple whitewashed,

An old Connemara barn, weighted against the wind.

Right: *an idyllic scene, Tory Sound, County Donegal.*

thatched-roof cottages, each with a little bit of land, set apart by fences made from piles of rock. The ruddy-faced Connemara folk eke out a living from farming on the rocky soil, tending sheep, fishing, and plying traditional crafts. Life can be hard inside these spartan cottages, yet there is always a cup of tea and a warm welcome for any and all strangers.

For fuel, families go out to the boglands to cut into layers of sodden earth and scoop out slices of rich brown turf. Invariably, they are accompanied by sturdy and sure-footed little donkeys pulling the turf carts home along the bumpy bog roads. Trees are scarce in Connemara, but those that do exist seem to be pointing in one direction, constantly swayed by the prevailing west winds off the Atlantic. The sounds of Connemara also hark back to an earlier time – rich, guttural intonations of the Gaelic language and the foot-tapping spirited tunes of Irish traditional music.

But Connemara is not the only place that conveys a picture postcard image of Ireland. Nearby County Mayo is equally bucolic. Mayo, in fact, is often called the country of *The Quiet Man* because it was the setting in 1951 for the classic film of the same name. In many respects, it hasn't changed much since then.

County Donegal, on the northwest coast along the Atlantic, is perhaps the most pristine of all Ireland. The Donegal landscape blends wide stretches of serene dune-filled strands with craggy rocks, sheer cliffs, deep valleys, snow-capped mountains, woodlands, lakes, rivers, narrow hairpin-style roads, and cascades of rocks that take on a warm, ruddy color at sunset. And in the midst of all of this sits Glenveagh, one of Ireland's most luxuriant national parks. Even the thatched cottages in Donegal are distinctive – the roofs are rounded, because the thatch is tied down by a network of ropes (sugans), fastened to pins beneath the eaves, so that the roofs are protected from the prevailing winds off the sea.

For those who never reach Donegal, there are still other places that epitomize the different faces of Ireland. Some people point to the gentle glens and wooded valleys of County Wicklow, others sing the praises of the pastoral hillsides of Counties Tipperary, Kildare, Carlow, Roscommon, or Longford. And no one can overlook the sparkling lakelands of Counties Cavan, Monaghan, Westmeath, or Leitrim; or the compelling isolation of Ireland's offshore islands, Achill off County Mayo, the Arans off County Galway, the Blaskets off County Kerry, and the Saltees off County Wexford. The list goes on and on.

Ireland is indeed a panorama, a collection of many experiences, different for each and every person, whether born to the soil or just passing by. No words can convey it better – the Emerald Isle is a treasure.

A bleak setting for a cemetery, Achill Island, County Mayo.

Above: *children in the surf in Bray, County Wicklow.*
Right: *modern farming in the Wicklow countryside.*

$\mathcal{E}$tchings of Time

In Ireland, the past is ever present. The country's history – long and glorious, yet often turbulent and troubled – is not just a chronicle of events confined to textbooks or museum displays. It is etched in the contour of the countryside.

At every turn, the story of yesterday is reflected – from ancient boulderlike dolmens and sky-high round towers to secret underground caves and circular stone forts, as well as multi-turreted castles and elaborately crafted cathedrals, sprawling monasteries and secluded manor homes, and simple beehive-shaped hillside huts and roofless abandoned stone cottages. Each structure, often side-by-side with today's prosperous farmlands and contemporary skylit bungalows, tells a different story of long ago.

Although Ireland is often overshadowed by the royal pageantry of Britain or the medieval architecture of France, Italy, and other neighboring countries, this island nation is no newcomer on the stage of European history. Dating back at least five thousand years, Ireland also easily surpasses America's five hundred years of recorded history ten times over.

Above: *ruins at Rawtoo in County Kerry.*

Indeed there is evidence of some human life in Ireland as early as 6000 B.C. or 8000 B.C., but most accounts focus on the period around 3000 B.C., the Neolithic or New Stone Age, a time when farmers, probably from Scotland, northern England, or the Isle of Man, settled in Ireland. Traces of their round or rectangular houses have been found in various parts of the countryside including Lough Gur, County Limerick, where some of these dwellings have been reconstructed and are now open to the public.

The most significant landmark of this period is a huge underground burial mound at Newgrange, County Meath, about thirty miles north of Dublin. Considered to be the finest remaining specimen of its kind in Western Europe, the Newgrange site contains a central chamber measuring 44 feet high and almost 280 feet in diameter, along with a passage 62 feet long. Excavations have not only produced the remains of Stone Age settlers, but also pendants, beads, and stones carved and ornamented with prehistoric motifs.

These early people also built dolmens, gigantic above-ground monuments, usually three or more standing stones covered by one large capstone. Still dotting the Irish countryside today, these huge boulders include the famous Poulnabrone, with a capstone of twelve feet by seven feet at Ballyvaughan, County Clare, and the Browneshill Dolmen in County Carlow, topped by a stone reputed to weigh over one hundred tons.

Throughout the rest of the countryside, amid mountain and coastal scenery, there are countless other relics from prehistoric times – ring forts (circles made of stone walls in diameters of up to two hundred feet), raths (small ruined fortresses), stone circles, standing stones, ceremonial mounds, and other earthwork remains. And when the original structures are no longer preserved, re-creations have taken their place, such as the "crannogs" or thatched-roof lake dwellings at Craggaunowen, County Clare.

By 1200 B.C., well into the Bronze Age, Ireland's early residents produced hoards of metal products, from bronze swords and cauldrons to an amazing variety of gold ornaments, such as gorgets, discs, rings, armlets, neck bands, and earrings. Many of these intricately designed items, said to represent the highest achievement of the goldsmith's craft in prehistoric Europe, have been unearthed in recent years and are on view at leading exhibitions, such as the National Museum in Dublin.

One of the longest-lasting cultural influences on Ireland began around 350 B.C. with the coming of the Celts from Continental Europe. The natives embraced

The Poulnabrone Dolmen, a chambered tomb that dates from Neolithic times, in the Burren, County Clare.

the Celtic way of doing things, from a language (Gaelic) which still survives today, to epic-style art, music, and literature. This was the age of horse-drawn chariots, local clans, provincial high kings, and larger-than-life heroes.

Every three years, it is said, a great national assembly (feis) of people from all over Ireland gathered on the Hill of Tara, a mighty mound overlooking the countryside in County Meath. Considered the cultural and religious capital of Ireland in ancient times, Tara was a powerful site – laws were passed, tribal disputes settled, and matters of peace and defense decided. As the old song goes, "The harp that once through Tara's halls, the soul of music shed. . . . " Today, however, Tara's halls are stilled, no turrets or towers, no moats or ceremonies. All that remains of Tara's former glory are memories and views of the Irish countryside from this awesome height, along with a few grassy mounds and occasional pillar stones.

Much of Ireland's folklore and traditional music traces its origins back to Celtic times. This period spawned some of the best-known tenets of Irish superstition, mythology, and legend, such as a place

Facing page: Aka Stone Circle – known as the "Seven Sisters" – in Killarney, County Kerry.

Mowing round a Megalithic stone circle at Carrowmore, a low hill in County Sligo.

called Tir na nOg, the land of youth; a woman identified as the banshee, one who wails when death is near; and, above all, the "little people" or fairies, elusive spirits in human form about six inches tall, and, in particular, the leprechaun, a fairy shoemaker said to have access to a pot of gold. It is likewise a firm principle of Irish lore that the three signs of beauty in a woman are a mole, especially on the neck;

Left: *digging for worms as the tide recedes on Bray beach, County Wicklow.*

Right: *Upper Lake in historic Glendalough, County Wicklow, the site of numerous fine ruins.*

Below: *swamp elder and heather cluster on the edge of a bleak lough in western Ireland.*

a fanis (faw-nish), the gap between two front teeth, and a large backside!

The Irish national psyche has also been significantly shaped over the centuries by Christianity, which arrived in the fifth century A.D. with the preachings of St. Patrick. The indefatigable saint is said to have traveled the length and breadth of the country – from the Hill of Tara to the smallest towns.

It was at Tara that Patrick plucked a three-leaf clover, or shamrock, from the grass to illustrate the doctrine of the Trinity. The spell-binding saint not only converted the High King Laoire to Christianity, but he also made such an impression on the assembled crowd that the shamrock has been synonymous with Ireland ever since.

Among the hundreds of other revered places where

Above: *a monarch butterfly, a rare visitor to Ireland.*

St. Patrick is said to have preached is the Rock of Cashel in County Tipperary, originally a royal fortress dating back to A.D. 360. Situated high on a two-hundred-foot outcrop of limestone above the town, the Rock was converted into a religious site in the twelfth century. Although in ruins today, it still dominates the countryside, with high vistas of a two-tiered chapel, cruciform cathedral, a ninety-two-foot-tall round tower, and a cluster of ancient crosses, tombs, monuments, and effigies.

No sooner had the Irish embraced Christianity, than they began to excel in spreading the word. Ireland's first written documents date from this period, produced at great monasteries and centers of learning that sprang up in such farflung locations as Glendalough in County Wicklow, and Clonmacnois in County Offaly. Princes, nobles, and prelates flocked from England and other nations for training.

The *Book of Kells,* an elaborate Bible produced in the late eighth or early ninth centuries, is the greatest remaining evidence of Ireland's leadership in such pursuits. Made of vellum, the pages are prized for

Below: *Virginia creeper, which brightens many a graceful Irish mansion in the fall.*

Facing page: *a silver brook curls through the countryside around the Ring of Kerry.*

their hand lettering and colorful illustration. The distinctively Irish script is bold and well rounded, semi-uncial in shape, while the artistic ornamentation flows with elaborate interlacing, fanciful abstract designs, and charming little animals, intertwined with foliage of plants and tendrils of vines.

For more than three hundred years, the *Book of Kells* has been on display in the Long Room of the Trinity College Library. Each day a new page is turned from among the 340 folios that survive. Much of modern Irish art and craftmanship has been inspired by this timeless thousand-year-old manuscript.

The same period produced the *Ardagh Chalice*, a huge religious cup, fashioned from a rich blend of gold, silver, bronze, and colored glass. It is considered the finest piece of eighth-century metalwork ever to come to light. Likewise the penannular *Tara Brooch*, thought to have been part of the personal adornment of a bishop, king, or queen, is particularly noteworthy for its gold filigree work. Like the *Book of Kells*, both of these treasured items survive and are on display in Dublin.

Facing page: *Celtic crosses, Glendalough, County Wicklow, Here extensive monastic ruins can be found in beautiful countryside.*

But such artistic bestowals are only teasers. Everywhere in the Irish landscape, there are reminders of Ireland's great attachment for Christianity – remnants and ruins of monasteries, abbeys, friaries, churches, cathedrals, and other farflung cloistered settlements of long ago. Some of these hallowed places are crumbled and roofless, but others still stand tall. One of the most frequent sights is the Celtic high cross, with over 150 specimens still dotting the countryside, including the often-photographed Cross of Muiredach at Monasterboice, County Louth; the Cross of the Scriptures at Clonmacnois, County Offaly; and the High Cross at Moone, County Kildare. Although they vary in style, most of these stone crosses are ringed with a circle at the juncture of the stem and arms. They are characterized by carvings that reflect a rich selection of biblical scenes, with figures shaped in high relief, grouped usually in twos and threes upon neatly framed panels or with a background of geometric patterns. All make a strong graphic, as well as religious, statement.

A pair of motorcyclists break their journey to investigate the past amid the stones of a ruined abbey in western Ireland.

Above: *the Round Tower at Rattoo, County Kerry.*

Left: *Glendalough's 1,000-year-old Round Tower, County Wicklow.*

Another legacy from early Christian times is the round tower, used originally as a campanile to call the monks to prayer. Standing erect to this day, these tall pencil-shaped stone towers, equivalent to five stories or more in height, are usually part of great monastic sites, such as Glendalough, a monastery of St. Kelvin at County Wicklow; Clondalkin, a monastery founded by St. Cronan in County Dublin; and Ardmore, a monastery of St. Declan at County Waterford.

In contrast, small beehive-shaped huts sit on the rocky hillsides of rural western counties. Built of unmortared stone, these watertight structures once served as individual cells or living quarters for monks, particularly those who led a contemplative and hermitlike existence. Originally, the huts were built in clusters around a church and surrounded by a stone wall, which cut off the outside world. Some of the best preserved beehive huts are in remote settings overlooking the Atlantic, such as the Aran Islands of County Galway or on the Dingle Peninsula and the Skellig Rocks of County Kerry.

In the same time frame, from A.D. 500 to 1000, as tiny Ireland drew scholars to its shores, it also sent missionaries abroad to educate students in all parts of Europe. To this day, the names of Irish monks are associated with religious sites throughout the continent, including St. Virgil (Salzburg), St. Colman (Melk), St. Kilian (Wurzburg), St. Martin (Tours), and St. Columba (Bobbio). This was the era when Ireland earned the title of "Isle of Saints and Scholars."

The days of glory were to be short-lived, however, as the Middle Ages also marked the beginning of an eleven-hundred-year period when Ireland would be raided, conquered, and dominated by outsiders.

The Vikings arrived first in the ninth century, initially plundering monasteries, the major centers of wealth and population, and then settling along the coast, establishing seaport towns at Dublin, Wexford, Waterford, Cork, and Limerick. In time, the natives united against the intruders and began to fight back. Led by Brian Boru, a local chieftain, the Irish won a major victory over the Vikings in 999, and subsequently Brian earned recognition as high king of all Ireland. A turning point came, however, in 1014 when Brian defeated the Vikings in the Battle of Clontarf, but perished in the process. For the next one hundred years, local provincial kings squabbled among themselves for power.

Late in the twelfth century, Dermot MacMurrough, a deposed local chieftain anxious to regain his authority, enlisted the aid of a band of warriors from western Britain. These new arrivals, known as Normans, were actually descendants of the same Viking invaders who had attacked Ireland and other lands three centuries earlier. They had settled in northern France, in the area known as Normandy, and hence they were called Normans when they eventually came to Britain with William the Conqueror. These Normans, first getting their feet on Irish soil by coming to MacMurrough's aid, ultimately conquered and prevailed in Ireland for hundreds of years, primarily in the guise of an Anglo-Norman relationship.

The Normans, however, were benevolent overseers, gradually intermarrying with the native population. It is often said that they became "more Irish than the Irish." Many names, common in Ireland today, can be traced to Norman origins, such as Barrett, Browne, Burke, Butler, Carew, Costello, Cruise, Cusack, Dalton, Darcy, Dillon, Fagan, Fanning, FitzGerald, Keating, Lynch, Martin, Power, Purcell, Roche, Russell, and Talbot.

Besides imparting their surnames, the Normans did a lot of building. They erected walls around major towns and cities, many of which remain at least in part today, and they built great churches and

Elegant Castlemartin mansion in Kilcullen, County Kildare.

Above: *a Ballyseede Castle window, Tralee, County Kerry.*

Left: *the mighty towers of sixteenth-century Dunmore Castle, which stands by the River Boyne in Navan, County Meath.*

cathedrals, but, most of all, the Normans are remembered for constructing castles. In fact, the majority of Ireland's castles still standing today had some Norman origins, from Malahide Castle, north of Dublin, owned by the Talbot family for eight centuries and opened to the public less than fifteen years ago, to such longtime tourist meccas as Bunratty Castle in County Clare and Blarney Castle in County Cork. Many castles, sometimes in ruins, continue to dot the countryside with moss-covered rectangular keeps, lichened rounded towers, and timeworn turrets.

A few outstanding specimens – preserved, restored, and glamorized – have been turned into luxurious resort hotels, such as Ashford Castle at Cong, County Mayo, originally the De Burgo (Burke) family residence, and Waterford Castle at Ballinakill County Waterford, home of the FitzGerald family for over eight hundred years. Other castles, influenced by the Norman style of architecture, were instead built

Left: *the view from a window seat in medieval Kilkenny Castle, County Kilkenny.*

Above: *the Long Gallery of Kilkenny Castle. Here hang pictures of the Butler family.*

by Irish chieftains. Two survivors in this category are both in County Clare – Dromoland Castle at Newmarket-on-Fergus, once the seat of the O'Brien clan and now a hotel, and Knappogue Castle at Quin, built by the McNamara clan and now a venue for nightly medieval banquets and entertainment.

Although the Normans left a distinctive and often dazzling mark on the face of Ireland, their coming also signaled a new wave of subjugation for the Irish. Recognizing the King of England as their overlord, the Normans embodied the first stage of the conquest of Ireland by neighboring Britain.

This chain of events lasted for over eight centuries,

starting in 1171, when King Henry II claimed power over Ireland, and extending until 1937, when the Republic of Ireland was finally recognized. The long chronicle of England's domination over Ireland, with its string of hardships and heroes, repressions and rebellions, conflicts and compromises, has filled hundreds of history books and still sparks many a heated debate.

In the end, Ireland has triumphed, at least partially. In spite of the continuing saga of Northern Ireland, the

Facing page: *restored thirteenth-century Kilkenny Castle, seat of the Butler family, on the banks of the Nore River, Kilkenny.*

Etchings of Time

Irish are now more fully masters of their own destiny than at any other time in recorded history.

Today Ireland and Britain coexist as neighbors, partners in trade, allies in business, and friends in word and deed. Britain sends more tourists to Ireland than any other country in the world, and, in turn, Ireland sends thousands of her talented young people to work in Britain year after year.

In so many ways, Britain's influence throughout Ireland remains to this day, most noticeably in the English language and shared traditions, in the style of government and laws, as well as in literature and theater. Many great masters of the language, such as Oscar Wilde, Jonathan Swift, George Bernard Shaw, and William Butler Yeats, divided their time between the two lands. Inevitably, the surnames of the British people who came to reside in Ireland over the years have gradually been accepted as "Irish." These names, often seen on shopfronts and in telephone directories throughout the country, include Acton, Allen, Andrews, Bailey, Buckley, Clifford, Collins, Cunningham, Eason, Farley, Hardy, Huggard, Hughes, Leonard, Loftus, Matthews, Moore, Newman, Parnell, Preston, Rossiter, and Smith.

Dromaneen Castle near Mallow, County Cork.

Facing page: *Marlfield House in Gorey, County Wexford.*

New-mown hay in Rathnew, eastern County Wicklow.   Right: *Muckross House, Killarney, County Kerry.*

Much of Ireland's architecture has also been shaped by Britain over the years, from Dublin's Georgian avenues, squares, and public buildings, to the countryside's varied selection of sprawling "big houses" or manor homes. Built by the Anglo-Irish aristocracy and absentee landlords, these great houses, dating from the seventeenth century, reflect the heyday of the "spare-no-expense" type of construction on a large scale.

More than forty structures, originally occupied by the rich and powerful, are now open to the public for everyone to enjoy. These include Castletown House, at Celbridge, County Kildare, a Palladian mansion built in 1722 for the Speaker of the Irish House of Commons; Muckross House, an 1843 neo-Tudor manor overlooking the lakes of Killarney; Emo Court at Emo,

County Laois, built in 1790 for the first Earl of Portarlington, and designed with a rotunda inspired by the Roman Pantheon; and the mid-eighteenth-century Georgian-style Bantry House in County Cork, built for the earls of Bantry and a repository of furniture and art from all over Europe.

As a testimony to the importance of tourism, some of Ireland's greatest houses have been transformed into country inns or luxury hotels. Adare Manor, County Limerick, a nineteenth-century, Tudor-Gothic mansion built for the earls of Dunraven, was opened as a hotel in 1988. With turrets, towers, barrel-vaulted ceilings, and fifty individually-carved fireplaces, this posh chateau is nestled on the banks of the River Maigue within a walled estate of 840 acres. One year later, an equally imposing hotel was unveiled at Mount Juliet, County Kilkenny, in a Georgian manor built in the late 1750s as a home for the eighth Viscount Ikerrin, first Earl of Cork. Situated along the River Nore in the heart of Irish horse country, Mount Juliet has its own stud farm as well as 1,466 acres of gardens and pastoral lands.

Dozens of other manor houses and country estates of varying size and splendor have found a new life as hotels, restaurants, or inns throughout Ireland, while hundreds of others remain in private hands. All of them, public or private, add much to the style and grace of the landscape.

Like the Normans, the English also were great castle builders. The benchmark of the castles that still remain is Lismore Castle, perched above the River Blackwater amid eight thousand acres of gardens and woodlands in County Waterford. Erected at the command of Prince John in 1185, this multi-turreted fortress is still in English hands, as the Irish home of the Duke of Devonshire, whose permanent residence is Chatsworth in Derbyshire. Although the castle itself is not open to the public, the luxuriant grounds are. In addition, at certain times of the year, the castle is also available for rent in its entirety, complete with staff. Nowadays, in times of rising castle-keeping costs,

The Haven Hotel in Dunmore East, County Waterford.

Right: *graceful Muckross House, County Kerry.*

anyone – titled or not – who can afford to pay a week's rent can be "lord or lady of the manor."

Gabled and mullioned Mallow Castle at Mallow, County Cork, built for the English Lord President of the province of Munster four hundred years ago, is now owned by an Irish-American and is also available for weekly rentals, as is the crenellated fairytale-style Glin Castle, overlooking the estuary of the River Shannon and home of the knights of Glin for the last seven hundred years.

So many other castles, erected at the behest of the English, are now landmark attractions of the Irish countryside, from the silvery towers of County Wexford's Johnstown Castle, to the Boyne River vistas of County Meath's Slane Castle, a Gothic Revival palace that was once the home of Lady Conyngham, paramour to George IV. Each castle is one-of-a-kind and each has a different story to tell, but they all contribute a touch of magic and romance to the aura that is Ireland today.

Surprisingly, even as Ireland remained under English influence, other nations left their mark on Irish soil. The Spanish, who had often docked their trading ships along the west coast, were particularly at home in Galway. Local lore claims that Christopher Columbus stopped in Galway as he set out on his voyage of discovery in 1492, and local placenames associated with Iberian visitors, such as the Spanish Arch and Spanish Parade, exist to this day. It is also claimed, perhaps with a somewhat tongue-in-cheek attitude, that many dark-haired Galwegians bear a resemblance to early Spanish visitors.

In 1601 Spain sent troops to help insurgent Irish

Left: *a statue in the gardens of Longueville House in Mallow, northern County Cork.*

Right: *flowering sherry glasses, Longueville House in Mallow, County Cork.*

Below: *a jaunting-car wheels by Muckross House, built in 1843 in Muckross, County Kerry.*

leaders, but the Spanish/Irish partnership was defeated by the English at the Battle of Kinsale. In a similar alliance, almost two hundred years later in 1798, the French put ashore to help the Irish at Killala, County Mayo, but were similarly thwarted.

Ireland's dramatic history has been influenced not just by other peoples, but also by the vagaries of nature. In the middle of the nineteenth century, the potato, long a staple of the Irish diet, was afflicted with a serious blight, and massive crop failure enveloped the land during the years 1845-1849, and again in 1851. Millions of people died of starvation or were forced to emigrate, leaving home without any hope of ever returning. Whole families just disappeared. Even today, roofless crumbling stone

Left: *Longueville House vines in Mallow, northern County Cork.*   *Thatched cottages in Adare village, County Limerick.*

cottages lie abandoned in remote areas of the Irish countryside, particularly in the counties of Kerry, Clare, Galway, Mayo, and Donegal, still reflecting the incalculable losses to the nation, as the country's population was decimated – slashed from a high of eight million in 1841 to under four million less than ten years later.

It was a heart-wrenching time for the Irish, as hundreds of thousands of people made their way to Cobh in Cork Harbour with little more than the clothes on their backs. Most embarked on torturously long journeys – to the United States, Canada, Australia, or New Zealand. Fortunately, most of them found a better life and prospered, forging the great links that contemporary Ireland enjoys with each of these countries.

Today, as an integral part of the European Community, Ireland is working toward a new closeness and relationship with all of the other member countries – Belgium, Denmark, France, Germany, Greece, Italy, Luxembourg, the Netherlands, Portugal, Spain, and the United Kingdom.

Undoubtedly, coming decades and centuries will bring more changes and new influences for Ireland. No matter what comes to pass, however, one thing is certain: Reflections of Ireland's glorious past and present will always endure and will forever meld with the horizons of a new tomorrow.

Facing page: *Rothe House,
which dates from 1594, in
Kilkenny, County Kilkenny.*

Right: *the historic windmill that
stands near the ship canal in
Blennerville, County Kerry.*

Below: *the ruins of a
coastguard station, Ardbear
Bay, County Galway.*

Above: *a fishermen's return, Glandore, County Cork.*
Right: *pines in silhouette at Aughanure, County Galway.*

The Land of Heart's Desire

It was William Butler Yeats, Nobel-Prize-winning poet and playwright, who first wrote the phrase "Land of Heart's Desire" to reflect the beauties and enchantments of Ireland. While Yeats intended to focus on his own County Sligo, his words are equally appropriate to describe all thirty-two counties.

For millions of people around the world, thoughts of Ireland touch the heartstrings in a compelling and often sentimental way. Immigrants and their descendents in far-flung countries yearn to go back, to see the land of their own heart's desire. "Come back to Erin," one famous song beckons. "Come by the Hills," says another. "Take Me Home" and "Come to the Bower" express similar feelings.

Other writers have chosen different phrases to convey an image of Ireland, from a "terrible beauty" to a "cloud in the west." Quite a few identify Ireland as a woman – "Cathleen Ni Houlihan," "Roisin Dubh" (dark Rosaleen), "Shan Van Vocht" (an old woman), a "mother of genius" or a "romantic lady." The paradoxes of Ireland – gentle yet strong, proud yet vulnerable – are all conveyed by these words.

Perhaps the most memorable phrases have been

Above: *early morning in an Irish garden.*

those that paint a vivid picture of the verdant land: "Forty Shades of Green," "Four Green Fields," "The Green Island."

For centuries, "green" has been just another way of saying "Ireland." Indeed no other country has such an instant identification with one single image. Ireland – idyllically and intrinsically green – fresh and natural, thriving and lush, pure and unpolluted. A paradise, indeed "a little bit of heaven," as an old song intones.

Think of it. Britain, France, Italy, Germany, nor any other European country can be summed up with one sweeping hue. Even the United States of America needs red, white, and blue to paint its image. But why is Ireland the "Emerald Isle," and not Greenland, nor Wales with its myriad green hills, nor Brazil with its many tropical rain forests?

The answer, of course, lies in the eyes of the beholders. For many, the first sight of Ireland is from the air. As an Aer Lingus jet prepares for landing, sweeping beneath the clouds, passengers see an unparalleled glimpse of Ireland unfolding below.

And, indeed it IS green. And not just a dull stretch of unbroken green turf – it is a maze of uneven and disparate green fields. Many are light in color with new growth, some are well cultivated and rich with crops, and others present a grassy vista rimmed with leafy trees. A few plots are large, while the majority seem like postage stamps from a skyward vantage point. Most are edged with hand-piled stone fences, dark gray dividers that accentuate the different shades of green in each field. Together, they form a palette of emerald hues, a patchwork quilt of Irish landscape.

Walls and wind-swept trees, Aughanure, County Galway.

A cow scorns ragwort by Doonagore Castle, County Clare.

And like a true patchwork, the expanse of the Irish countryside is rich in ornamentation. The rounded stacks of hay look like tawny gum drops on the hillsides, and the major roads appear to be thick black threads as they curve through the open countryside, winding past craggy mountains and rippling lakes. The tableau is dotted with neat little whitewashed cottages, compact farmsteads with tin-roofed barns, crumbling ruins of once-mighty fortresses, occasional restored castles, and endless herds of nomadic sheep and grazing cows.

Thanks to the frequent but gentle rains, and the warming influence of the Gulf Stream, Ireland is always green, even in the depths of winter. The trees may lose their leaves, but the fields are forever green.

Green, too, are the trimmings. Leafy shrubs meander along the roadways deep into the open countryside. The sharply pointed leaves of the holly bush, the sprawling branches of the rhododendron, the graceful fronds of palm, and countless others, are all equally at home edging the seascapes of Kerry, the boggy plateaus of Connemara, the sheltered lakes and valleys of Wicklow, or the mountain trails of Donegal.

In spring and summer, the greens gladly share the limelight with a rainbow of colorful blooms – golden bristles of gorse, overlapping stalks of lavender-toned heather, tender red teardrops of fuchsia, creamy bell-shaped clusters of arbutus, and the hooded deep purple flowers of the greater butterwort.

Even the Burren country of Clare, swathed with barren sheets of rock, is surprisingly and wondrously ablaze with wildflowers in May and June. Forcing their way out of the shallow soil through a maze of crevices and fissures, these stubborn plants, often thought to be of Arctic-Alpine origin or even survivors from the Ice Age, range from deep blue spring gentians and small mustard-colored rock roses to sprawling snow-white mountain avens and the unique dense-flowered orchid, a lime-and-cream-colored, upright cluster of blooms.

Flowers and greenery are everywhere in Ireland – in the front yards of private homes, in public spaces, along the roadsides and by the sea. Some of the most varied assortments of flowers are in historic garden parks, now open to the public, but originally the private estates of the wealthy Anglo-Irish aristocracy.

Above: *Marlfield House in Gorey, County Wexford.*

Right: *romantic Tory Sound, northwestern County Donegal.*

Above: *a kniphofia, or red hot poker, in Kenmare, County Kerry.*

Bouquets wrapped for sale on a Dublin flower stall bring summer to the city.

Right: *thatch and marigolds in the pretty village of Adare in County Limerick.*

Even Dublin, the bustling capital city, is alive with gardens and parks of exceptional beauty. Foremost is Phoenix Park, Europe's largest urban park (1,752 acres) on the city's western edge. Traversed by a network of roads and pedestrian walkways, it is landscaped with ornamental gardens, seasonal flowers, nature trails, broad expanses of grassland, avenues of trees, and pasture lands. Among the handful of buildings in this park are the residences of Ireland's president and of the United States ambassador.

Just south of Dublin, on the east coast, is County Wicklow, an area so lush with foliage that it is commonly referred to as "the garden of Ireland." And in a country universally acclaimed for its verdant pastures, that's quite a tribute to Wicklow. It is a county of rhododendron-lined country lanes, wildflower-rich glens, thickly wooded valleys, and crystal-clear lakes, all within sight of domed granite mountains and sandy seascapes, and dotted with white-washed, well-kept little towns with fanciful

Stern statues and cheerful petunias stand beside a lily pond in immaculate Powerscourt Gardens, the pride of County Wicklow.

names like Annamoe, Ballinalea, Glencree, Kilmacoo, Laragh, and Shillelagh.

Enniskerry, County Wicklow, is the home of Powerscourt Gardens, long regarded as one of the most splendid horticultural estates in Europe. Set beside the River Dargle, Powerscourt is a grand formal garden in the traditional sense, with wide sweeping terraces, ornamental lakes, antique statuary, decorative iron work, a park with herds of deer, and a waterfall, the highest in Ireland, tumbling from a four-hundred-foot cliff.

In stark contrast is the compact setting of bonsai trees, topiary, and lily ponds at the Japanese Gardens at Tully in neighboring County Kildare. Situated on the grounds of the Irish National Stud Farm, these gardens offer an unexpected look at the art of Japanese-style landscaping in the heart of Ireland's horse country. Laid out between the years 1906-1910, they symbolize "the Life of Man."

Although many people don't believe it until they see it, subtropical vegetation thrives in Ireland, particularly in the southwest, thanks to the warming effects of the Gulf Stream. Palm trees are one of the

most surprising sights, but magnolias, camellias, and other warm-weather shrubs are equally at home. One of the greatest clusters of subtropical flora grows on Garnish Island, also known as Ilnacullin, in Bantry Bay, accessible only by boat from the palm-tree-rimmed town of Glengariff in west County Cork.

Conceived and planted in 1910-1913 by Harold Peto, the gardens are laid out in an Italianate design with pedimented gateways, a Martello tower and a clock tower, and a Grecian temple overlooking the sea. Floral specimens from many continents blend and blossom on this balmy island retreat, so atypical of the usual notion of Irish landscape. No wonder local lore maintains that George Bernard Shaw sought refuge and inspiration on Garnish Island when he was writing *Saint Joan*.

Another of County Cork's islands, Fota, is distinguished for its arboretum, started in 1820. Less than ten miles east of Cork City, Fota seems to float in a world of its own, far from the bustle of urban life, although it does have great links with all parts of the

Left: *a blush pink rose, one of many in Powerscourt Gardens, County Wicklow.*

High summer in an Irish country garden, typical of Adare, County Limerick.

earth. Trees and shrubs from every continent have taken root on Fota, ranging from Huon Pine from Tasmania, to a handkerchief tree from China.

Ireland's newest arboretum is the John F. Kennedy Park at Dunganstown, County Wexford, opened in 1968 and dedicated to the memory of the thirty-fifth president of the United States. Set on the southern slope of Slieve Coillte overlooking the late president's ancestral home, this six-hundred-acre expanse is home to five thousand species of plants, trees, and shrubs, including over five hundred different rhododendrons, one hundred fifty types of azaleas, and a collection of eucalypti.

Flowering magnolias, cherries, and crab apples thrive in the gardens of Birr Castle, County Offaly, in the heart of Ireland's central farmlands. Dating back over three hundred years, this one-hundred-acre display contains over a thousand different species of trees and shrubs, which are laid out around a lake and along the banks of two adjacent rivers with waterfalls and riverside walks. It is a serene and majestic setting, befitting a castle, with avenues of maples, chestnuts, weeping beech, and giant box hedges that are considered to be the tallest in the world.

The wealth of the gardens in Ireland is proof, of

Rugged Glengarriff, County Cork, a valley which is thought to have one of the most genial climates in all Ireland.

Rainbows come to an end on both banks of the River Suir in Waterford city. An international festival of light opera is held here every year.

course, that Irish weather is a mix of frequent rain and ample sunshine, and not just a shroud of perpetual mist. And even if gray clouds do dominate the skies on many days, a rainbow often follows.

The rains may dampen some activities and try the patience of serious photographers, but, on the whole, rains are expected, almost taken for granted, and even welcome in Ireland. Imagine if it didn't rain in the Emerald Isle – all the characteristic greens would soon fade. And besides, the clouds do keep moving. If it's raining in Cork, chances are that the showers are already over in Killarney.

There are several old Irish weather predictions that can be quite accurate as well as humorous: "If it's not raining, then its about to rain," or "If you can see the mountain encircled with clouds, then it's about to rain; if you can't see the mountain, then it is raining already," or "If you don't like the weather, wait five minutes, and it will change."

In fact, Ireland's cloud formations add much to the landscape. Even on sunny days, puffs and wisps of clouds are constantly moving in off the Atlantic, across the country from west to east. Sometimes the clouds are bunched up or clustered together, foretelling of imminent rain, but often they are independent streaks of white dancing across the azure skies.

When clouds are at their best, they are not too high in the sky, either in the early morning or late afternoon, and they do not totally obscure the sun. At

such a time, take a stroll to the edge of one of Ireland's rivers or lakes, perhaps the lower lake at Killarney. Stand at the edge of the waterline and breathe the sweet air, scented by the nearby arbutus and holly bushes. If the wind is calm, the lake is a mirror. The puffy clouds, fringing the tops of mountains and hovering over the ancient leafy trees, are all reflected in the silvery blue waters, perfectly still like a masterful painting. Alas, scenes such as this don't last very long, but they do remain forever in memory.

The variety of the Irish landscape also makes an indelible impression. Although most people think of Ireland as being quite flat and boggy, the entire coastline is ringed by mountains. They may not be as impressive as the Alps or Rockies, but they are craggy, curvy, and full of character. Sometimes they are not called mountains at all, but are known by Irish language names that mean mountain or peak, such as "Ben" or "Slieve" or "Croagh."

The tallest mountain, Carrauntuohil, at 3,414 feet, is part of the MacGillycuddy's Reeks range on the Ring of Kerry in the southwest corner of Ireland. The

Right: *a patchwork of rock and pasture, County Cork.*

Right: *a magnificent view from Healy Pass, a mountain pass that marks the boundary between Cork and Kerry.*

Below: *a Dunmore East cottage, County Waterford.*

99

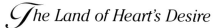

mountains of Kerry have a particular beauty and boldness. Often shrouded in cloud, they almost seem to be blue or purple in color, adding to their domineering stance on the horizon.

Mount Brandon, with a rugged face of natural cirques and steep hollows, rises above the Atlantic shoreline on the edge of the Dingle Peninsula to a height of 3,127 feet. The country's second highest mountain, also in County Kerry, it served as a dramatic backdrop for the 1970 film, *Ryan's Daughter*.

Lugnaquilla, at 3,039 feet, is Ireland's third highest mountain and the tallest outside of County Kerry. It sits amid the lush foliage and myriad lakes of County Wicklow, casting gentle shadows on the Vale of Avoca, the Vale of Clara, and legendary Glendalough.

Some of Ireland's most impressive peaks have literary connections. Ben Bulben, a flat-topped, 1,730-foot mountain in County Sligo, provided constant inspiration for William Butler Yeats. At his request, Yeats is buried five miles away in Drumcliffe Churchyard "under bare Ben Bulben's head."

Croagh Patrick in County Mayo is one of Ireland's "holy mountains," a site of annual religious pilgrimages. It is said that in A.D. 441 St. Patrick prayed on the summit of this 2,510-foot mountain and spent the forty days of Lent there. Traditionally, over the last fifteen hundred years, Christians have returned to this height to do penance and honor Ireland's patron saint.

Far up the coast, in the rugged northwest, is Mount Errigal at 2,466 feet. Often capped with snow, this gentle mountain stands out in the County Donegal

Left: *walled but still wild: the Ardbear Bay shoreline, western Connemara, County Galway.*

A beach on Tory Sound, one of the finest and most unspoilt in County Donegal.

Above: *tranquil Dunmore East, County Waterford.*   Below: *Graiguenamanagh swans, County Kilkenny.*

Rain over the Caha Mountains, County Kerry.

skyline with its cone-shaped summit and rocky gray face, surrounded by low-lying boglands.

Ireland's other mountains have definitive names, such as the Bluestacks, Blackstairs, Devil's Bit, and Hungry Hill, while some have more lyrical appellations, like Galtee, Caha, and Knockmealdown. A few are known solely by their Irish language name – Slieve Snacht (Mountain of Snow), Slievenamon (Mountain of the Women), Slieverue (Russet Mountain), and Benbaun (White Mountain Peak). In all, they combine to make an undulating edge around Ireland, sort of like a bumpy ridge around a saucer.

Beneath and beside the mountains, Ireland's landscape is a veritable potpourri of hills and glens, plains and plateaus, some rocky and some rich with fertile soil. Much of Ireland, indeed one-seventh of the entire land mass, is bogland – vast blankets of sponge-like red-brown turf, also known as peat.

Fondly referred to as the "wild fabric of the island," the bog has long been an intriguing facet of many parts of the Irish countryside. It is spread over the central plain in counties such as Offaly and Laois, as well as throughout the coastal lowlands and highlands of Kerry, Donegal, and Mayo, and especially in Connemara, County Galway, where over a third of the land is bog. It is a unique surface, flat but uneven,

103

An interplay of light and shadow over Ardbear Bay in Connemara. The Twelve Bens that dominate this region can be seen beyond the hills overlooking the bay.

Above: *peat-cutters break for lunch on a peat bog and, naturally, use a fire of this age-old fuel to heat water for their tea.*

almost buoyant, and the roads that traverse the boglands are inevitably bumpy and tiresome.

What exactly, people often ask, is a bog? It's a huge chunk of land, varying in size from a couple of acres to a few square miles. Usually a former lake basin or shallow pond, it has been filled in over the centuries, by parts of decaying trees, plants, mosses, stones, rains, mists, and more – a murky composite of earth and water. A bog can be a little like quicksand, engulfing whatever lies in its path. When the bog is settled and can be walked upon, small pieces of sod can be sliced from the ground and stacked to dry in the sun. The result is a chunk of turf, a natural and efficient source of fuel. Making a fire from turf for cooking or for warmth is common practice in Irish homes, particularly in rural areas. As it burns, the turf

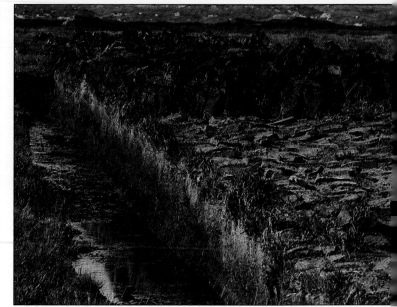

106

Facing page bottom: *peat left to dry in County Galway.*

Above: *Connemara men and their cattle on the way home.*

emits an earthy – almost sweet – aroma and sends blue wisps of smoke up the chimney. The distinctive smell of turf and the blue spirals of smoke are two unmistakable emblems of the Irish countryside.

Rock, just plain ordinary rock, takes up a lot of space in the Irish landscape. If rock were worth just a tenth as much as diamonds, it has been said, Ireland would be one of the world's richest countries. These Irish rocks, of course, are no gems.

There is so much rock, wedged into the soil of the western counties such as Galway, Mayo, Donegal, Kerry, and Clare, that it is sometimes difficult to imagine how any crops grow. But, the Irish, being optimists at heart, have coped well with their rock-strewn fields. They have literally sifted through the land, setting boulder-like rocks aside, and made workable soil, often by adding seaweed and sand to the earthy mixture.

They use dislodged rocks for practical purposes, like building fences to enclose their small tracts of land. Many of these fences are literally rock and nothing else, no mortar or cement. These rock fences are the result of a perfect balancing act, painstakingly put together by wedging rock upon rock. Many of the stone fences, or stone hedges as they are often called, have survived centuries of wear and tear, wind and weather. These rocky pilings stand firm, as testaments to the bare-handed and backbreaking work of generations of Irishmen, who have eked out a living from the stone-encrusted land.

Bleak as the rock-rimmed horizons can be there is always the refreshing and cooling contrast of the sea. As an island, Ireland is surrounded by water – no part of this little country is more than seventy miles from the sea.

Cattle browse on a Connemara smallholding in sight of the Twelve Bens. The living here is not easy, the land being either boggy or rocky and never very fertile. The views, though, are awesomely beautiful.

Waterville homes defy the sea, County Kerry.

The whirling waters of the Atlantic Ocean, joined by the Irish and Celtic seas, surround the three-thousand-mile coastline of Ireland. Beaches and strands, from Rossnowlagh to Rossbeigh and Banna to Brittas – long and glorious stretches of firm silvery sand, hold diversions and delights for all.

And who can overlook the gentle waters of Ireland's briny bays, from the storied Bantry Bay to Galway Bay, celebrated equally for its sunsets and

oysters, as well as those with unforgettable names and views to match, such as Roaringwater Bay, Ballycotton Bay, Blacksod Bay, and Clew Bay?

The spell of the sea is indigenous to Ireland – in the truest sense, it goes with the territory. And, even within Ireland's innermost regions, hardly a mile goes by that there isn't some hint of a stream, a brook, a lake, a lough, a waterfall, or a river. The soothing sounds of a ripple or a splash are invariably within earshot.

The River Shannon alone stretches over three-

Above: *the unspoilt Fanad Peninsula, County Donegal.*   Below: *limestone, heather and gorse, Connemara.*

Left: *County Kerry pastureland, renowned for its richness.*   *Western Ireland, "land of the mountain and the flood."*

quarters of the length of the land, making it the longest river in Ireland or Britain, while smaller rivers, such as the Blackwater and Boyne, also meander for miles over several counties. Just about every major Irish city is positioned on the banks of a river – Dublin on the Liffey, Cork on the Lee, Waterford on the Suir, Wexford on the Slaney, Kilkenny on the Nore, Sligo on the Garavogue, Ballina on the Moy, and Donegal on the Eske.

Originally used as avenues of transport, Ireland's rivers today also serve as sources of power and natural outlets for recreation and fishing. And the lakes or loughs take up where the rivers end, reaching out into all parts of the countryside.

In all, there are more than one thousand rivers and lakes on this tiny island. Some are celebrated in poetry and song like Killarney's three lakes, referred to as "heaven's reflex" and "beauty's home," and the lake Isle of Innisfree and Lough Gill in Yeats' works, but most of the lakes just sparkle and shimmer, like cool blue freckles on the incomparable face of Ireland. 113

Above: *Siamsa, the National Folk Theater of Ireland, in Tralee, County Kerry.*
Right: *drying the washing in County Kerry.*

*W*ealth of Words and Music

In Ireland words are like gemstones, always cherished and constantly being polished. Whether words are spoken, written, sung, dreamed of, or mused over, they are treasured equally in the bustling cities as well as on the bucolic farmlands.

It was G.K. Chesterton, on a visit to Dublin over seventy years ago, who said that the city was a "paradise of poets," declaring that half the Irish talked in verse. Indeed speaking well and speaking lyrically is second nature to the Irish.

Fascinated by language, the Irish seem to be always talking. And well they should, for they have at least two languages from which to draw substance and inspiration. While it is true that most Irish people speak English, many are also fluent in their own native language, Irish or Gaelic.

This ancient vernacular is basically a Celtic language, related to Scottish Gaelic, Welsh Breton, and ancient Gaulish. Dating back more than a thousand years, this was the predominant language of the people well into the seventeenth century, until English overshadowed it.

Above: *Kilkenny women passing the time of day.*

Many of Ireland's place names are derived from the Irish language. The original meanings, shown in parentheses, are descriptive of each place. Killarney, from Cill Airne (church beside the sloe tree); Cork, from Corcaigh (marshy place); Limerick, from Luimneach (bare spot); Sligo, from Sligeach (shelly place); Knock, from Cnoc (hill); Glendalough, from Gleann Da Loch (glen of the two lakes); Kinsale, from Ceann Saile (tide head); Tramore, from Tra Mor (great beach); Clonmel, from Cluain Meala (honey meadow); Mayo, from Maigh Eo (plain of the yew tree); and Donegal, from Dun na Gall (fortress of the foreigners). Most road signs bear the English and Irish names of cities and towns.

Today, although fewer than one hundred thousand people use Irish for everyday communication, it is a language that is widely revered and closely associated with the intrinsic "Irishness" of Ireland. To ensure that the use of Gaelic is not diluted or assimilated into English, Gaelic speakers do not spread themselves too thinly throughout the country, but instead live primarily in the west, clustered together in "Gaeltacht" or Gaelic-speaking regions.

The largest Gaeltachts are in rural parts of Donegal, Galway, Mayo, Kerry, and Cork. During the past one hundred years, serious efforts have been made to encourage growth and economic well-being in these areas. The goal is to preserve the Irish language for many reasons, not the least of which is its great tradition of oral history and storytelling. Indeed the art of telling a story, either in Gaelic or English, has long been synonymous with life in Ireland.

A thousand years ago, a person who could speak well, and especially recite tales or poems, was welcomed everywhere, even in the company of kings. A good storyteller, called a "seanachie" (shan-ah-kee´) by the Irish, was expected to know more than two-hundred-fifty long tales and at least another one hundred lesser tales. Some stories took five minutes to an hour in the telling, others would stretch over three nights.

A good storyteller's repertoire would include tales of battles and wars, travels and adventures, magic and mystery, romance and rivalries. People are said to have followed the tales with the same fervor that characterizes twentieth century soap opera devotees.

Although greatly diminished in this century with competition from radio and television, the verbal art of storytelling still thrives and thrills, particularly at family or community gatherings. Even in New York or London or Auckland, when an Irishman is called upon to sing or entertain at parties, he will often opt to tell a modern-day tale. Not a joke or a riddle, but just a well-spun and well-spoken story.

Dancers wait their turn to entertain in Dublin town center.

Facing page: a rosy dancer, red from effort but smiling, in Dublin.

No matter what language they are using, the Irish are never at a loss for words. In many ways, words are the lifeblood of the Emerald Isle. Some people say that this tendency to chat at the drop of a hat is the result of an innate curiosity about anything new or different, while others claim that the Irish are just naturally friendly. It is probably a blend of both.

Travel the roads of Connemara or Clare, Donegal or Dingle, and the experience is the same. Encounter an Irishman on the road and ask for directions. He will not only provide a detailed commentary on all the surrounding roads and turns, but he will invariably ask a few questions as well. In the end, he will probably interrupt what he is doing and offer to lead the way himself.

It is not surprising that people who have such a

in Irish, however, has been an uncial-style script, although the English alphabet is now used interchangeably.

Some of Ireland's greatest poetry and prose, written in Irish from the eighth to the seventeenth centuries, survives to this day. A large number of the earliest pieces are short poems with emphasis on nature and the sights and sounds of the sea, sky, and land. The longest poems tend to be of epic proportions, recounting the deeds of Ireland's high kings. The prose is equally varied, from the sagas of early Irish heroes, such as Cuchulainn and Finn MacCumhaill, to great historic annals, or the mythological tales about the fairies or the "little people."

Ireland's most noticeable impact on the literary world, however, has been in the genre of Anglo-Irish literature (writings by Irish men and women in English). A majority of these works, created in the last three hundred years, were penned by Irish-born writers who spent most of their adult life outside of Ireland, usually in England or Europe.

They chose to live outside of Ireland for various reasons, not the least of which was to be close to major publishing houses and theaters. Inevitably, Irish-born writers also found more freedom to write what they wanted by going abroad. Many Irish writers have been ahead of their times and mores, or perhaps too critical of established systems. Although they were often embraced as geniuses abroad, their works were initially censored or banned at home in Ireland. With the passing of time, however, most all these literary exiles eventually earned both approval and respect in their homeland.

The contributions of these writers, both individually and collectively, continue to have a strong impact throughout the world today. Indeed critics have often wondered aloud how a country as small as Ireland could generate such an abundance of significant writing.

The names read like a literary who's who from Jonathan Swift, the master of satire, and Oscar Wilde, the incomparable wit, to Ireland's three Nobel Prize winners, George Bernard Shaw, William Butler Yeats, and Samuel Beckett, as well as Oliver Goldsmith, Richard Brinsley Sheridan, Thomas Moore, James Stephens, George Russell (AE), George Moore, Oliver St. John Gogarty, and James Joyce, the maverick novelist who forged new and unprecedented styles of writing.

Even Ireland's great political heroes, such as Robert Emmet or Patrick Pearse, wrote or spoke memorable and evocative words when they faced death. Pearse left oft-quoted poems behind, and Emmet's "Speech from the Dock" has been immortalized as a national rallying cry. "When my

Mid-hop – Morris dancers entertain in Dublin.

love of speaking embrace the written word with equal vigor. The earliest known written form of Irish or Gaelic is "Ogham," a stick-like script dating mainly from the fifth and sixth centuries. Examples of Ogham writing can still be seen on ancient stones throughout the countryside. The predominant format for writing

Dublin's Concert Hall, which has superb acoustics.

country takes her place among the nations of the world," he said, "then, and not till then, let my epitaph be written."

As the home of the Abbey, the Gate, and dozens of other theatres, Ireland is also known for its compelling drama, both classic and experimental, including works by John Millington Synge, Sean O'Casey, Brendan Behan, Brian Friel, John B. Keane, and Hugh Leonard. These are but a few of the best-known names.

Hundreds of other writers, both past and present, have also left their mark, both in Ireland and beyond its shores.

Best of all, contemporary Irish writers do not have to go abroad to earn recognition and acceptance. New ideas are welcomed, controversy is relished. The atmosphere in modern Ireland is conducive to creativity, and the writer is a revered figure. There has even been a literary about-face, with authors from other lands, including the United States, coming to Ireland to live and write. At various times, the Irish

Irish dancing at Dingle Fair, County Kerry.

government has even extended tax incentives to encourage more writers to be in residence.

Music is also endemic to this misty and lyrical island. As a people often conquered and oppressed, the Irish have always found music to be a source of joy and self-expression. Wherever the Irish gather – be it by a hearthside, in a pub, or at a crossroads, music is bound to result.

Along with most of Europe, Ireland can trace its musical beginnings back to the bards of medieval times, who traveled the countryside singing songs and telling tales, usually to the accompaniment of a harp. So important was such music that the harp was adopted as part of the coat of arms of Ireland in the seventeenth century and remains the official symbol of the country to this day.

Although this bardic music was seldom written down, the works of one such poet, harpist, and composer, Turlough O'Carolan, have survived and provide the basis for many modern-day airs and ballads.

In addition to the mellow and lilting music descended from the bards, the bulk of Irish music is robust and zesty, fast-paced and foot-tapping in style, played on an array of instruments. One of the most effervescent is the uilleann pipe (pronounced: ill'-un), a form of bagpipe pumped with the elbow in a sitting position. Often referred to as the "Irish organ," it produces a more resonant sound than its Scottish counterpart.

Other components of Irish music are the accordion (sometimes called the concertina), fiddle, flute, tin whistle, and the bodhran (bow'-rawn), a hand-held drum which can best be described as a goat-skin tambourine. The Irish have also been known to improvise and use anything from a wash board to a set of spoons to make music.

The inventory of Irish music is enormous – happy ditties and sad airs, romantic melodies and war tunes, songs of struggle or celebration, ballads extolling heroes or deprecating fools, lyrics with a message and some just for a laugh. Very often, Irish music sings the praises of Ireland, from such universally-known tunes as " Dublin's Fair City," "Galway Bay," and "The Hills of Donegal," to local favorites such as "The Kerry Dances," "Bantry Bay," "The Old Bog Road," "When It's Moonlight in Mayo," and "The Rose of Mooncoin."

Some of the most memorable Irish music is meant for listening, such as the airs and melodies played by the Chieftains or by flautist James Galway. Audiences around the world, from Canada and California to China, have been enchanted by these ambassadors of music, while throughout Ireland other lesser-known but equally dedicated players bring similar sounds to hundreds of festivals and community gatherings.

Any excuse at all is a good enough reason for music – and all kinds of music. As the home of internationally acclaimed rock stars such as U2, Ireland vibrates with contemporary music. The country is also host to an array of world-class annual music festivals – classical music in Dublin, opera in Wexford, light opera in Waterford, jazz in Cork, choir music in Sligo, marching bands in Limerick, country music at Lisdoonvarna, and folk music in Killarney.

Music is everywhere in Ireland – in the homes, the schools, the pubs, the theaters, the streets, the open countryside, and, especially in the hearts of the people.

Above: *a pot of geraniums: Limerick simplicity.*
Right: *sheltering sheep on the Aran island of Innishmore.*

Enduring Crafts

Wildflower mauve, shamrock green, seawave blue, granite gray, rhododendron red, and bogland brown. These are the unmistakable colors of the Irish countryside, and they are also the inspiration for Irish tweed.

One of Ireland's oldest crafts, the weaving of tweed by hand has long been a mainstay of Irish creativity and livelihood, especially in the remote parts of the countryside. Each bolt of Irish tweed, painstakingly produced at small factories and in individual homes, is as distinctive as the weavers and looms that produce it.

Donegal tweed, from the northwest corner of Ireland, is a sturdy and complex fabric, characterized by nubby textures and speckles of diverse colors. It mirrors the vistas of the rugged and windswept County Donegal landscape.

This robust tweed is much in demand for suits, coats, and jackets, as well as traditional peaked walking caps. The weather-resistant caps, worn by just about every man in Ireland – and much sought after as souvenirs by visitors – seem to last a lifetime.

Equally prized tweeds are woven in other parts of Ireland as well, especially in Connemara and Wicklow. Ireland's oldest hand-weaving company, dating back to 1723, still thrives amid a cluster of stone buildings at Avoca in County Wicklow.

The Avoca tweeds, softer in texture than the Donegal patterns, are rich in lighter colors – the pinks,

Above: *man of the West, an Aran Islander.*

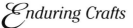

heathers, and teals of County Wicklow's gardens. These tweeds are fashioned into capes, coats, ponchos, suits, and jackets for women, as well as bedspreads, blankets, and rugs.

Ireland's success as a tweed-producer is due not only to the talent of her people as weavers, but also to the countryside's suitability as pastoral land, ideal for raising sheep and other grazing animals. Sheep thrive in every Irish setting, from the rich grassy fields of Wexford and Kilkenny to the rocky hillsides of Mayo or Clare. Drive around the country and it seems as though sheep are everywhere, meandering on lonely trails, huddling on windy plains, perched on the edge of mountain peaks, and indeed often dodging traffic in the middle of busy roads.

Thick with wool, Irish sheep also provide the raw material for yet another traditional Irish craft – the knitting of chunky oatmeal-colored Aran fishermen's sweaters. These garments owe their name and their beginnings hundreds of years ago to the Aran Islands, three remote and rocky islands off the coast of Galway. Surrounded by the waters of the Atlantic Ocean, the Aran Islanders had little source of income except for fishing off their coasts in small leather-made boats called currachs.

The fishermen, often battling churning waves, stormy winds, and driving rains, needed protective clothing for their long hours at sea. Responding to this mighty need, the women of the islands knitted with strong, heavily oiled wool, guaranteed to repel the effects of the elements. They not only knitted sweaters, but also jackets, trousers, caps, and stockings.

Left: *sheep safely graze in Mallow, County Cork.*

Marigolds gone to seed beside an old croft in Western Ireland.

Facing page: *ewes and their lambs enjoy a late summer's afternoon in pastures green near Mallow, County Cork.*

Right: *beef cattle fatten on rich grazing land in southwestern Ireland. Irish beef is some of the tastiest in Europe.*

Below: *fine-looking ewes and lambs in County Cork, soon to be shown, no doubt, at the local agricultural show.*

Above left: *a weatherbeaten cottage faces the sea on Inishmore in the Aran Islands.*

Above: *a lop-eared goat takes his ease on a windswept morning in Western Ireland.*

Left: *a splendid set of horns on an Irish billy goat, worthy of a puck goat at Killorglin's annual Puck Fair in County Kerry.*

Over the years, certain families of knitters developed distinctive stitches and patterns, many of which are still used today. These stitches include the shapes of a honeycomb, ladder, trellis, cable, basket, diamond, moss, and fern. It is said that if a fisherman drowned at sea and was washed ashore, the best way of identifying him was by the pattern of stitches in his knitted clothing.

With increased links and regular travel between the islands and the mainland in the twentieth century, visitors began to purchase Aran knit sweaters for fashion as well as practicality. Knitters in Connemara,

parts of Donegal, and Mayo also began to produce the garments in their own homes.

In recent years, hand-knitting has become a burgeoning cottage industry in all parts of Ireland. Weeks of time, exacting detail, and great pride go into each garment. When a sweater is finished, each knitter affixes a tag with her own name, an action compared to signing a work of art.

Often imitated but never equalled, every Aran hand-knitted sweater is unique – a one-of-a-kind creation, shaped by the skills and personality of its maker as well as the time-honored tenets of the craft.

Wildflowers line a single track road beside well-established fields in Western Ireland, much of which has remained essentially the same for centuries.

𝓔nduring Crafts

Like fine wool products, linen is also synonymous with Ireland. It is said that the growing of flax for linen can be traced back to Bronze Age times. Indeed there is evidence that linen was often used for hangings in medieval monasteries and for the tunics of the early Irish kings and queens, although it was the damask variety, introduced three hundred years ago, that brought international fame to Ireland as a linen-producer.

Irish linen damask tablecloths have become known the world over for their distinctive patterns, many of which reflect the graceful swirls and shapes of Ireland's foliage, flowers, and even shamrocks. In recent years, there has been a revival of interest in Ireland's fine linens, particularly in the fashion industry.

Even more exacting is the artistry required for the Irish craft of lace making. Universally prized for its nimble-fingered stitchwork, Irish lace has varied little since it was introduced in the late sixteenth or early seventeenth century. Delicate wedding veils, doilies, and tablemats are usually full of traditional patterns of the fern, shamrock spray, and wildflowers.

Centered in the homes or convents of Limerick, Kenmare, and Carrickmacross, lace making is still primarily a cottage industry, with skills passed slowly from one generation to the next.

Above all, the craft most readily identified with

A mongrel dog prepares to greet the photographer on one of the Aran Islands, where bleak fields stretch to the horizon.

Facing page: stylized flowers and leaves form an intricate pattern in handmade lace, for which Ireland is world famous.

Above: *a gaily painted cottage, almost Mexican in appearance, in Inistioge, County Kilkenny.*

Facing page: *gray walls and sky brightened by a blanket of golden thatch and a cheerful red door in County Sligo.*

Right: *a dilapidated cottage in Doolin, County Clare. Such dwellings are reminiscent of the Irish peasants' cottages of the nineteenth century.*

The magnificent crystal chandeliers that hang in the reception hall of Waterford Glass Works, Waterford city, County Waterford.

Ireland undoubtedly is crystal – glittering and glistening handcut glass. The oldest and foremost of all Irish crystal companies is, of course, Waterford, founded in 1783, closed in 1851 as a result of the ravages of the famine years, and happily revived in 1947. It is also the largest glassware factory of its kind in the world, providing a choice of over sixteen hundred different items, ranging from napkin rings and pendants to chandeliers and golf trophies. In recent years, however, other handcut crystal operations have begun to flourish in various parts of Ireland, particularly in Galway, Cavan, Tipperary, Sligo, and Dublin.

In every case, it takes finely honed skills and years of training to produce this exquisite glass. Veteran glassblowers begin this process by lifting fiery balls of molten glass onto iron rods from the depths of huge furnaces. They use only their breath, artistic instincts, and wooden blocks to transform these white-hot masses into traditional glassware shapes.

Intricate patterns, named after Irish people, places, and things, are later cut into the glass by teams of master craftsmen. They work strictly from memory, with meticulous precision and dexterity.

Each finished piece is a classic of craftmanship. It is not surprising that handcut crystal glassware from Ireland adorns some of the world's most hallowed chambers – from Dublin Castle to Westminster Abbey, the White House, and Independence Hall.

Right: *crystal door handles at Tinakilly House in County Wicklow. The strength of crystal is clearly demonstrated by using it for this purpose.*

A craft that is newer to Ireland but one that requires equal skill is Irish Dresden, a line of porcelain figurines produced at Drumcollogher, County Limerick. These delicate pieces are fashioned in the tradition of a business originally founded in Volkstedt, Germany, and brought to Ireland over thirty years ago. Four-hundred-year-old German master molds are used by a team of fifty potters, artists, and designers to turn out new patterns inspired by life in rural Ireland.

Similar Irish porcelain and pottery crafts are practiced in all parts of the Emerald Isle. Two of the leading names are Royal Tara China in Galway, which uses patterns reflecting Irish history, and Donegal Parian China in Ballyshannon, which employs designs depicting Irish flowers, vines, and the shamrock.

Great impact on the craft of traditional Irish jewelry design has been made by the Claddagh ring. First developed in the sixteenth century by a goldsmith from the ancient village of Claddagh on

Enduring Crafts

Galway Bay, this simple ring features a pair of hands holding a crowned heart.

Primarily used as a wedding ring by the people in the west of Ireland, the Claddagh ring is now worn throughout the world and has come to be accepted as a universal symbol of friendship, love, and loyalty.

Other leading Irish crafts include basketry, heraldry, batik, patchwork, stained glass, beaten copper art, wood carving, doll making, enamel painting, pewter casting, bookbinding, and candle making, to name only a few.

On the practical side, the craft of thatching is one of the household arts of the Irish countryside,

Left: *a small brass bell glows against mahogany in Tinakilly House, County Wicklow.*

Right: *haymaking, when all the family helps to gather the crop before the weather breaks.*

Below: *a smoking chimney on a snug Aran Islands croft belies the sunshine's promise.*

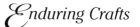

particularly in the remote rural western counties. The style of putting a thatched roof over a whitewashed stone cottage goes back hundreds of years in Ireland, to a time when only the rich and powerful could afford slates, tiles, or other imported materials. The poor farmers and workers had to make do with local materials, such as reeds, rushes, grass, flax, and straw made from wheat, rye, oat, or barley sheaves.

Today the same natural materials are still used, each carefully selected, dried, matched for size, and then woven in place and secured by a network of ropes, pins, pegs, or wisps of straw known as bobbins. The precise methods of laying thatch vary from one part of Ireland to another, but all types of this work require great skill and patience to achieve a long-lasting, weather-resistant finished product. Because of modern-day insurance concerns, however, other roofing materials are fast replacing the thatch. Sadly, it seems that thatching is becoming a dying art, although many parts of the country are making concerted efforts to preserve this time-honored tradition.

Although it is not strictly a craft, one of Ireland's most famous products is whiskey. In fact, the Irish are credited with inventing whiskey distilling.

The story goes that Irish monks concocted the first

*A Border collie lies out of the
wind in the Rosses of County
Donegal. The Rosses are a
lake- and rock-strewn district
that stretches along the
Atlantic coast from Dungloe to
Innishfree Bay.*

brew for medicinal purposes in the sixth century. These same monks carried the recipe to Scotland. They called their invention "uisce beathe" (pronounced: ish'-ka ba'-ha), which in Gaelic means "the water of life"; shortly afterward, it was Anglicized to "whiskey." In 1608, a license to distill alcohol was granted to Old Bushmills, making it the world's oldest distillery still in operation.

Irish whiskey differs from Scotch or English whisky in the method of distillation. The Irish use a combination of local malt and unmalted barley, which is allowed to dry naturally without the aid of heat and smoke, while the Scottish-English mode of distilling requires the use of smoke-dried malted barley. The result gives Irish whiskey a clear, smooth, and smokeless taste.

Most Irish whiskey today is brewed at a central distilling plant located at Midleton, County Cork; it has the largest pot still in the world with a capacity of thirty-three thousand gallons.

Another Irish brew of great renown is Guinness stout, a black, yeasty ale with a foamy head. The Irish

Above: *Ballyporeen, County Tipperary, the ancestral town of Ronald Reagan.*

Left: *securing haystacks against those fierce County Donegal gales in Derrybeg.*

Right: *dolphins cavort amid brass waves on a Wexford town door knocker, an indication of Wexford's long maritime tradition.*

like to drink it on draft in a large tumbler glass called "a pint." Sipping a pint of Guinness is the favorite pastime in the pubs, and has been since this dark beer was first produced in Dublin by Arthur Guinness in 1759.

With such creations to their credit, it's easy to understand why George Bernard Shaw equated Irish hearts with pure imagination. Inspired by Ireland and its traditions and resources, the Irish people have added much to the world.

143

Above: *waiting to see the favorite walk out at the Curragh,
County Kildare.*
Right: *the finest of Irish thoroughbreds do battle at the Curragh.*

Passion for Sport

*The Irish are a competitive breed. And that makes sport, in all its forms, a
year-round national obsession. Even the major newspapers pay homage to
sporting stories, placing soccer results and racing forecasts on the second and
third pages of daily editions, right after the main headlines.*

The sport of choice, for young and old, rich and
poor, blue-collar worker and blue-blooded aristocrat,
is horse racing. Nothing warms the heart or quickens
the pulse of an Irishman like the sight of a frolicking,
frisky horse.

In legend and lifestyle, the horse has always been
synonymous with Ireland. No one knows exactly when
the first horse galloped across the open plains of
ancient Ireland, but folklore is rich with tales of
chariot racing by the legendary Irish hero Cuchulainn.

Tradition also holds that in the middle of the third
century A.D. horse racing was well established at the
Curragh, still the country's major track. By the
seventh century, the Irish horse was an indispensable
part of life, often depicted in such works as the *Book
of Kells*, showing horsemen riding bareback using
bridles but no saddles nor stirrups.

Above: *Bantry, at the head of
Bantry Bay, County Cork.*

44

Usually alluded to as the sport of kings in medieval times, horse racing in Ireland today is truly the sport of the people. There is racing almost three hundred days a year, rotating among twenty-eight racetracks, some with state-of-the-art glass-enclosed facilities, such as the Curragh of Kildare or Leopardstown in Dublin. Others, like Tralee and Tramore, Galway and Gowran, are simple, grassy patches with open-air seating or standing. At Laytown, County Meath, the horses gallop along the sandy surf-edged beach as spectators watch from nearby hillsides.

Most of all, contemporary racing in Ireland is a social experience, a chance to greet old friends, to make new acquaintances, to see and to be seen. Some races, like the Irish Derby at the Curragh, are dressy occasions, with hats and finery as handsome as any ever worn at Churchill Downs, Ascot, or Longchamps.

Of course, there is wagering at the windows, but the beehive of activity for serious gamblers is the "betting ring," a trackside area where fast-fingered bookmakers chalk up the odds on their portable blackboards and make payouts from oversized

Facing page: silks and feathers in the saddling enclosure of the Curragh, County Kildare.

Below: the winner returns after a race at the Curragh racetrack, County Kildare.

Above: *serious talk at Lisdoonvarna racetrack, County Clare.*

briefcases. For many, it's worth a trip to the races just to try and outsmart the "bookies," sometimes more respectfully known as "turf accountants" or "betting agents."

In addition to racing, there are at least five hundred other horsey events held in Ireland each year, from the open fields of the smallest villages to the grandstands of major cities. Children, who learn to ride almost as soon as they can crawl, take pride in grooming their own horses or ponies and competing at local fairs and national events. Ever since 1864, the benchmark of all these gatherings has been the Dublin Horse Show, a five-day, mid-summer program of show jumping, dressage, exhibits, animal sales, and parties galore.

During the months of November through March, some of the focus shifts to Ireland's famous hunt clubs, such as the Galway Blazers, the Tara Harriers, and the Scarteen Black and Tans. Riders decked out in

Facing page: *a brood mare and foal, Western Ireland.*

Above: *Ireland's calcium-rich grazing, ideal for horses.*

traditional gear – red or black jackets, sturdy peaked caps, buff britches, and high boots – mount the horses of their choice and take to the chase. Led by a local hunt master and a pack of eager beagles, the hunting team pounds across the open fields in search of the wily fox, undeterred by stone walls, ditches, double banks, or streams. Sounds of "Talley-ho!" ring out through the countryside – nothing adds more luster to a wintry Irish landscape. And, after a day's outing, fox or no fox, everyone adjourns to the local pub for some animated chatter and cheer.

Over the years, the Irish horse has evolved into a priceless national asset, not only for racing, riding, and hunting, but for the more practical tasks of transport and farmwork, as well as a unifying symbol and source of inspiration. Indeed nothing enhances a drive through the Irish countryside more than the sight of a lush green field full of horses, each well-groomed and markedly individual, with a pelage of either raven black, chestnut brown, titian red, cloud white, or misty gray.

Stop and watch a horse, any horse, as it struts, swaggers, and sashays. Strong-boned and full of stamina, the Irish horse is all-at-once patrician and peerless, yet playful and perky. The mares stand out, graceful and guarded, leading their foals into the open spaces, nudging and encouraging their offspring to run and romp in the grassy pastures.

Today Irish horses are the focus of a multi-million-dollar bloodstock industry. There are more than three hundred stud farms spread throughout the countryside, particularly in the fertile rolling hills of Tipperary, Limerick, and Kilkenny, and the limestone-rich plains of Kildare. Bloodstock sales take place year-round throughout the country, attracting buyers from all over the world as well as many who come just to admire these magnificent animals in the flesh.

In typical Irish style, horses are esteemed even long after they have died. The skeleton of Arkle, one of Ireland's most famous steeplechasers of the 1960s, is the most popular exhibit at the Irish Horse Museum at Tully, County Kildare, while the grave of The Tetrarch, known as "the spotted wonder" for his racing speed, has been a revered site for over fifty years in the grounds of the sylvan Mount Juliet Estate in County Kilkenny. Even the bar at Mount Juliet is named after The Tetrarch, and the walls are lined with the names of many other prize-winning horses raised on the estate in the last one hundred years. In nearby Tipperary, the heart of horse country, there is a small town aptly named Horse-and-Jockey.

Equestrian activities are only the beginning of the Irishman's (and woman's) love of sport. In this country known for many shades of green, there are, not surprisingly, nearly two hundred golf courses. And when it comes to teeing off to the emerald fairways, the Irish seem to have golf in their genes.

The game is played by men and women of all ages and walks of life, from scientists to secretaries and farmers to philosophers. Indeed it has been said that the Irish may not have invented the game of golf, but they have certainly perfected it.

With so many courses, the Irish rarely have to wait or endure long lines to play. A round of golf is a weekend ritual for most Dubliners or Corkonians, while the country folk find an excuse to play on any day that the weather gives them enough encouragement. In the summer, with daylight stretching until 10 P.M. or 11 P.M., many Irish golfers look forward to a full eighteen holes after work.

The Irish play golf as the game was meant to be played – any time of year, rain, shine, calm or wind, and usually without mechanized equipment or showy gear.

Ireland's golf courses are as varied as the landscape itself – some courses wind around mountains or along rivers, others overlook valleys or lie under palm trees, and many are within the confines of cities or at farflung resorts.

Lahinch, nestled near the Cliffs of Moher on the Atlantic coast of County Clare, has two courses, one of which is considered to be the Irish circuit's most challenging championship layout. Often called the "St. Andrews of Ireland," it is the paradigm of Irish links golf, with open vistas of rocky hillsides, roaring waves, windswept dunes, and ancient ruined castles. Originally conceived by Tom Morris, this course was updated under the guidance of Dr. Alister MacKenzie, whose other designs include the Augusta National Course, home of the United States Masters tournament.

Ballybunion, rated as one of the world's finest by Tom Watson, has recently added a second eighteen

150 | *Fine bloodstock out to graze in Croom, County Limerick.*

holes, designed by Robert Trent Jones, Jr., to its beach dune setting in County Kerry, while a new course designed by Arnold Palmer has opened nearby on the sea's edge at Tralee.

One of Ireland's longest courses is on the scenic Ring of Kerry at Waterville, laid out on 7,234 yards of lofty sand dunes and bounded on three sides by the Atlantic. Referred to as "the beautiful monster" by Sam Snead, this is one of the few courses in the Emerald Isle where motorized golf carts are allowed.

On the east coast just north of Dublin, Portmarnock sits on a spit of land between the Irish Sea and a tidal inlet. First opened in 1894, this eighteen-hole championship links has been the scene of many an international tournament. This course, along with the neighboring Royal Dublin, are but two of over thirty golf venues that meander between the mountains and the sea beside the capital.

Whether an Irish golf course is near the heartbeat of a major city or deep in the furrows of the countryside, one thing is for sure. Every club has its

own version of the "nineteenth hole," each with its own particular ambiance.

Perhaps no sport is more in tune with the gentle ebb and flow of the Irish lifestyle than salmon or trout fishing. To cast a rod on one of the more than a thousand Irish rivers or lakes is to enter a world set apart, to slow down, relax, and forget pressures. Listen to the splash of the water, the hum of insects, the rustle of reeds, perhaps the song of a skylark, or the bleat of a mountain sheep. A fisherman stands alone, silent, at peace. It's the Irishman's version of yoga!

And if all of this seems too serious, the Irish angler is bound to win a smile by reciting the designations of the colorful man-made flies that usually woo the salmon – names like silver doctor, blue charm, dusty miller, and hairy Mary.

Where to fish in Ireland is never a problem. The Ballynahinch system in Connemara and the river valleys of the Blackwater, Barrow, Corrib, Moy, Nore, and Suir are particularly known for dependable salmon catches. Sea trout fishing (classified as salmon by Irish fishery officials) is at its best in the shorter coastal streams of the Waterville Fishery in County Kerry as well as in the myriad waters of Connemara, Mayo, and Donegal. Brown trout, the most common

Facing page: *small craft tie up at Courtown, County Wicklow, a popular holiday resort favored by families.*

Rowing boats out of reach of the lapping lake in the Killarney Lakes region of County Kerry, Western Ireland.

An ordered row of yachts that have found safe mooring at Dunmore East, a small angling resort which lies at the mouth of Waterford Harbor in eastern County Waterford.

155

Small craft at Greystones near Wicklow, County Wicklow.

Right: *serene water, Wexford town harbor, County Wexford.*

and widely distributed of Irish freshwater fish, is found in every stream, brook, lake, and river including the Shannon.

Ireland also enjoys a long tradition of sailing, dating back to 1720 with the foundation of the Cork Water Club, now known as the Cork Yacht Club, the oldest yacht club in the world.

No round-up of Irish sports would be complete without mention of Ireland's traditional Gaelic games. Hurling, one of the world's fastest sports, is played with two teams of fifteen, using wooden sticks and a small leather ball. Gaelic football, also played by two teams of fifteen, is a field game similar to rugby or soccer except that the ball is round and can be played with the hands.

With huge followings in Ireland's thirty-two counties, these all-amateur sports are played every weekend throughout the summer, culminating in September with the All-Ireland Finals, an Irish version of the "Super Bowl."

The list of sports in Ireland goes on – from currach or canoe-style open-boat racing off the coast of Galway and road bowling in parts of County Cork, to snooker and soccer, clay-pigeon shooting and cricket,

billiards and hot-air ballooning, not to mention "going to the dogs" at a greyhound race.

But if there's one thing that the Irish love more than playing, watching, or betting on their sports, it's talking about them. In such a small country, it is readily understandable that all sports endeavors are big news. Olympic contenders like Ronnie Delaney, Eamonn Coghlan, and John Tracey are forever national heroes. When Ireland reached the quarter-

finals for the world soccer cup in 1990, the whole country was engulfed in animated discourse about the fledgling Irish team. Thousands of people from all parts of Ireland, led by the country's Prime Minister, flew to Italy to voice their support. And even though the Irish team did not return home victorious, the determination and talent of the players and their manager remained a hot topic long after the event.

Similarly, the names of champion horses and the statistics of their big races can usually be recited by young and old alike. Hardly a week passes that some sporting event is not the focus of everyday conversation – by the firesides, at offices, on the farms, in the shops, during recesses at schools, and, most of all, in the pubs. It seems that everyone has an opinion and everyone is involved.

But that's the Irish – if they can't be part of the action, at least they can expound on it.

Above: *blue eyes and black hair – coloring typical of the Celt.*
Right: *one of Ireland's favorite modes of transport, Waterford.*

*L*asting *Impressions*

Ireland's greatest asset is her people.
No doubt about it. No second guesses. No ifs, ands, or buts. It's a fact, proven time and time again.
As breathtaking as the multi-green scenery is, as awe-inspiring as the castles may be, or as thrilling as picking a winner at the Irish Derby can be, nothing tops the natural charms of the people. No matter how much the sun shines, how often it rains, or how many rainbows suddenly appear, it is Ireland's people who make the lasting impressions.

Nothing else can compare to an Irishman's or Irishwoman's way with words, quick wit, genuine friendliness, and inherent ability to comment about everything under the sun. "Having a chat," an Englishman once remarked, "is the great Irish hobby."

And making time for a chat is second nature to the Irish. No business, no transaction, no bargaining can ever be completed without a bit of a chat – a close encounter of the human kind.

It is little wonder that Ireland's greatest export has always been her people. From the days of St. Patrick, the Irish have set forth to change the world, first to Christianize it, and then to blaze new trails, chart new frontiers, start new lives. In the United States alone, the Irish have spread their influence from coast to coast – more than forty million Americans claim Irish ancestry. Even the White House was designed by an

Above: *one of Ireland's sons – a lad from the West.*

Irishman, James Hoban from Carlow. Of the forty-one United States presidents, fourteen have been of Irish stock.

But it's the Irish who remain at home in Ireland who impart the intangible open-hearted feeling that envelops the country. These are the people who give meaning to the song "When Irish Eyes are Smiling." It doesn't take long to notice that a smile comes as naturally to the Irish as taking a breath.

No matter how hectic their lives are, or how harsh the elements are around them, the Irish can always find time for a gesture of goodwill to friend and stranger alike. "Fine day, isn't it?" they will say in passing, even as dark clouds loom on the horizon.

Drive the open roads and watch the farmers saving the hay, stacking the turf, or tending their sheep, or the neatly uniformed children walking home in bunches from school. Invariably, they will stop for a moment to wave at a passing car, whether they know the occupants or not. If their hands are busy with shovels or spades or armloads of books, at least there will be a nod of the head or a wink of the eye. Even in the big cities, a smile comes much easier to the Irish than a scowl or a stare.

Left: *"when Irish eyes are smiling …."*

Below: *Waterford's mine of tourist information.*

Because Ireland is such a small country, everybody knows everybody else, or at least they know of one another. It's a kind of "national familiarity" that holds true equally within the hubbub of the cities and amid the tranquility of the countryside. This compulsion to know and be known can best be summed up in the old Irish adage, "There are no strangers, only friends we've yet to meet." Quite simply, people are genuinely interested in one another, and, for visitors, this translates into a very friendly and congenial atmosphere.

To express the warmth of their welcome, the Irish usually employ the Gaelic words, "Cead mile failte" (which means "One hundred thousand welcomes"). Not one or two welcomes, or even a few dozen – only a hundred thousand will do. Hospitality is de rigueur for the Irish.

With this inherent proclivity toward socializing, it is plain to see why the Irish love their pubs. Indeed, for centuries the pub has been a focal point in Ireland – a common ground for people of all walks of life, all religions, all political persuasions.

In many ways, the growth of pubs has been a direct reflection of Irish lifestyle. The origin of pubs harks back to a time when there were no hotels or restaurants. In those days, neighbors would gather in a country kitchen, often to sample some home brew.

As a certain spot grew popular, word spread and people would come from many miles, always assured of a warm welcome.

Such places gradually became known as "public houses" or "pubs," for short. In time, the name of the person who tended a public house was mounted over the doorway, and hence many pubs still bear a family or proprietor's name, such as M. Ryan in Dublin, Aherne's at Youghal, Paddy Burke's at Clarinbridge, or Moran's of Kilcolgan. Others have names that pertain to aspects of Irish culture or everyday interests – from the Piper's Chair in Doolin and Farmer's Kitchen in Wexford, to the Silver Salmon in Kinsale, The Thatch at Ballisodare, and The Matchmaker at Lisdoonvarna. In remote areas, many pubs often doubled as general stores or pharmacies, and today some publicans still sell groceries, leather goods, and household supplies.

Thousands of Ireland's pubs have been in the same family for generations and have changed little in the last two hundred years. A few may have added television, pool tables, and dartboards to their decor, but the true Irish pub is still basically a homey place – a unique hybrid of a warm fireside, a news depot, and a gathering spot for refreshment of all kinds, including spontaneous music and just plain good conversation.

An unassuming bar in Glendore, County Cork.

Lasting Impressions

No wonder there are over ten thousand pubs on this tiny isle – the Irish pub is both a national institution and a common denominator thoughout the land.

If there is one place that an Irish man or woman cherishes even more than a pub, it is the hearth. Rare is the Irish home that doesn't have a fire glowing in the fireplace, even in the summer months. The distinctive peaty aroma and blue spirals of smoke that signify a turf fire are as endemic to the Irish countryside as the green hillsides and woolly sheep. And sitting beside each and every fireplace, there is always a tea kettle, warmed and ready.

In the humblest or grandest of homes, it is a tradition to offer "a cuppa" – a cup of tea – to anyone who should appear at the door, expected or not. And it is likewise a tradition to accept the offer, thirsty or not. No matter what the hour of the day, along with the tea invariably comes a piece of bread or cake, and, above all, a chance to sit by the fire and chat.

"When God made time, he made plenty of it," the Irish are fond of saying. And it is a phrase that pretty much sets the pace for living in the Emerald Isle. Rushing or conforming to the clock is not part of the Irish way of doing things.

Appointments are kept in business circles, of course, but a few minutes off the mark are seldom noticed. If a dinner party is set for 7.30 P.M., rarely would any considerate guest arrive before 8 P.M.. About the only time that the Irish accelerate is when they are behind the wheel of a car – and then they go

Tea time, Bennettsbridge, County Kilkenny.

Right: *Paddy Burke's, pride of Clairnbridge, County Galway.*

Left: *refreshment at Longueville House, an eighteenth-century Georgian mansion in Mallow, County Cork, which today does service as a luxury hotel.*

Right: *firemen deal calmly with a smoldering stack of hay in Western Ireland. Such fires are common when damp hay is stored, since it will ferment, raising the temperature in the center of the stack to the point when a fire breaks out.*

like demons. They drive fast because they know every turn of the road and they like to aim for the speed limit, not because they are serious about beating the clock.

For a visitor, winding down to to the local come-what-may pace is important in Ireland, because one never knows what will happen next. It may look like a wet day in the morning, but sun will usually streak the skies by afternoon. The pub may be quiet early in the evening, but by dark it will be filled with rollicking music and good-humored fun. The restaurant may appear to be a simple cottage, but inside reigns a Cordon Bleu chef. The farmer with the tweed cap may seem shy at first, but say two words and the conversation is off and rolling. Being prepared – and eager – for the unexpected is the secret of being Irish.

In the long history of the country, this ability to adapt and change with the circumstances has been fundamental to the Irish. Even though they were dominated by outsiders for centuries, the Irish never gave up, never dimmed their smiles. They clung to their traditions, sought the bright spots, stretched out the happy times. To this day, the Irish never want a good party to end. If they are having a merry time – singing, laughing, making music, and storytelling – then the Irish will stay up well into the night without a yawn or a single tinge of regret for lost sleep.

Ah, the spirit – and the stamina – of the Irish. No words can fully capture the essence of Ireland's people, and their ability to glean from the past, revel in the present, and speculate on the future. Indeed the Irish are unique.

And so it follows that Ireland, a constant reflection of her people, is truly like no other land on this earth.

Above: *strong colors and simple designs characterize the architecture of Passage East, County Waterford.*

Left: *a ship-shape house in Passage East. This attractive village stands high above Waterford Harbor and was at one time fortified.*

Facing page: *the round tower at Ferrycarrig looms over the River Slaney in County Wexford. It is thought to be part of the first Anglo-Norman castle to be built in Ireland.*

Right: *brothers in mischief – lads from the west of Ireland pause in their play for refreshment.*

Facing page: *swans inspect a rowing boat on the River Barrow at Graiguenamanagh in County Kilkenny.*

Below: *an antiques shop cat scowls at the camera in Glandore, County Cork.*

Above: *a Kenmare lass smiles through a shower in County Kerry.*

Right: *thatched houses, reminiscent of fresh-baked loaves, lie close together at Glencolumbkille, a historical village in County Donegal.*

Above: *youngsters rejoice in bad behavior at the Puck Fair in Killorglin, County Kerry.*

Facing page: *fishing in the Liffey from a precarious perch in the center of Dublin.*

Left: *sisters stop to smile. In large Irish families, the elder daughters often stand in for mum while she works.*

Facing page: *a dense forest of conifers. The Irish government has effected extensive afforestation schemes.*

Below: *thatch gone to seed covers a weatherbeaten store near Lahinch in County Clare.*

175